ANAGRAM
CHALLENGE
Over 240 puzzles to do anywhere, anytime

How to use this book

In **Anagram Challenge**, you use the letters provided in the puzzle to find the one seven-letter word and other six-, five-, and four-letter words that can be made using those same letters.

The central letter of the puzzle (always shown in grey) must be found in all the words, no matter how long they are. Each puzzle has a series of fill-in boxes – one letter per box – so you can keep track of your answers. The answer boxes are listed in alphabetical order from top to bottom, left to right.

Easy and Medium puzzles have some clue letters given, to help you find the right words. Expert puzzles have no clues – you are on your own!

We have not included less common words in the solutions, but well done you if you come up with a word that is not included. Give yourself an extra point for your super vocabulary skills!

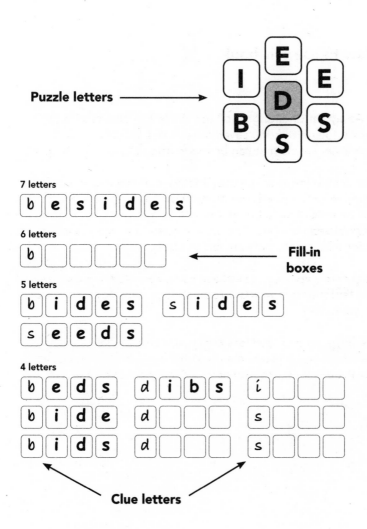

Puzzle letters

I E E
B D S
S

7 letters
b e s i d e s

6 letters
b ☐ ☐ ☐ ☐ ☐   ← **Fill-in boxes**

5 letters
b i d e s   s i d e s
s e e d s

4 letters
b e d s   d i b s   i ☐ ☐ ☐
b i d e   d ☐ ☐ ☐   s ☐ ☐ ☐
b i d s   d ☐ ☐ ☐   s ☐ ☐ ☐

Clue letters

Puzzle 1

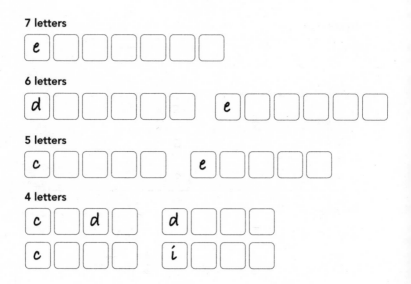

7 letters

e

6 letters

d   *e*

5 letters

c   *e*

4 letters

c   *d*   *d*

c   *i*

Puzzle 2

7 letters

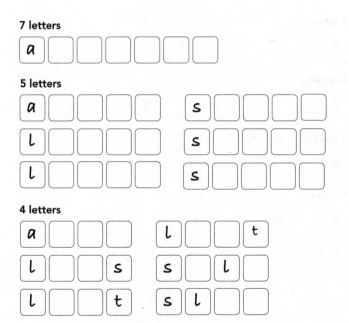

5 letters

4 letters

Puzzle 3

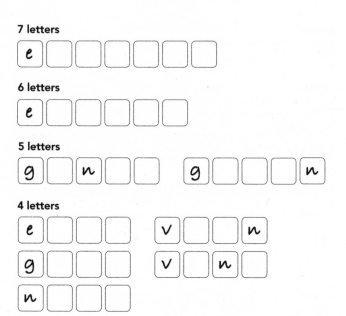

7 letters

| e | | | | | | |

6 letters

| e | | | | | |

5 letters

| g | | n | | | | g | | | | n |

4 letters

| e | | | | | v | | | n |

| g | | | | | v | | n | |

| n | | | |

Puzzle 4

7 letters

b _ _ _ _ _ _

5 letters

b _ _ _ _   c _ _ l _

c _ _ _ l

4 letters

a b _ _   b _ n _

b _ l _   b _ a _

Puzzle 5

7 letters

c _ _ _ _ _ _

5 letters

c _ _ _ _   u _ _ _ _

s _ _ _ _

4 letters

a _ _ _   s _ u _

g _ u _   s _ n _

g _ n _

Puzzle 6

7 letters

6 letters

5 letters

4 letters

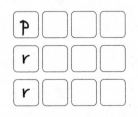

Puzzle 7

7 letters

e ☐ ☐ ☐ ☐ ☐ ☐

6 letters

e ☐ ☐ ☐ ☐ ☐

5 letters

b ☐ ☐ ☐ ☐   b ☐ ☐ ☐ ☐

b ☐ ☐ ☐ ☐

4 letters

a ☐ ☐ ☐   b ☐ ☐ ☐

b ☐ ☐ ☐   b ☐ ☐ ☐

b ☐ ☐ ☐   b ☐ ☐ ☐

b ☐ ☐ ☐   n ☐ ☐ ☐

b ☐ ☐ ☐   s ☐ ☐ ☐

Puzzle 8

7 letters

k ☐ ☐ ☐ ☐ ☐ ☐

6 letters

k ☐ ☐ ☐ ☐ ☐

5 letters

d ☐ ☐ ☐ ☐   k ☐ ☐ ☐ ☐

d ☐ ☐ ☐ ☐   s ☐ ☐ ☐ ☐

i ☐ ☐ ☐ ☐   s ☐ ☐ ☐ ☐

4 letters

d ☐ ☐ ☐   i ☐ ☐ ☐   s ☐ ☐ ☐

d ☐ ☐ ☐   k ☐ ☐ ☐   s ☐ ☐ ☐

d ☐ ☐ ☐   k ☐ ☐ ☐   s ☐ ☐ ☐

i ☐ ☐ ☐   k ☐ ☐ ☐

11

Puzzle 9

7 letters

b

5 letters

a

b

c

s

4 letters

b

b

b

c

c

c

s

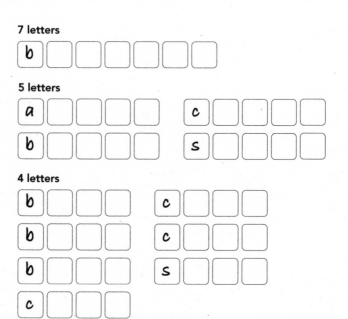

Puzzle 10

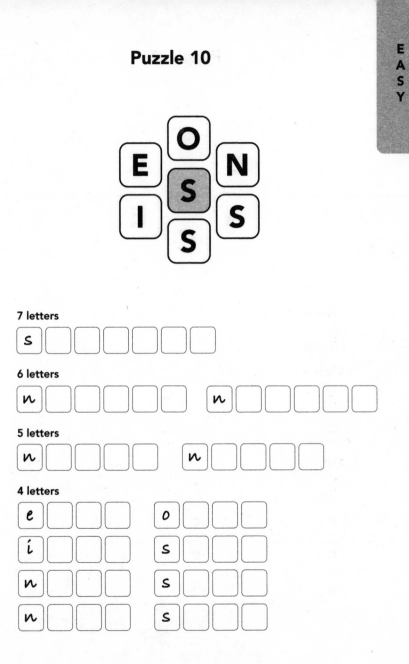

7 letters

S

6 letters

n

n

5 letters

n

n

4 letters

e

o

i

s

n

s

n

s

Puzzle 11

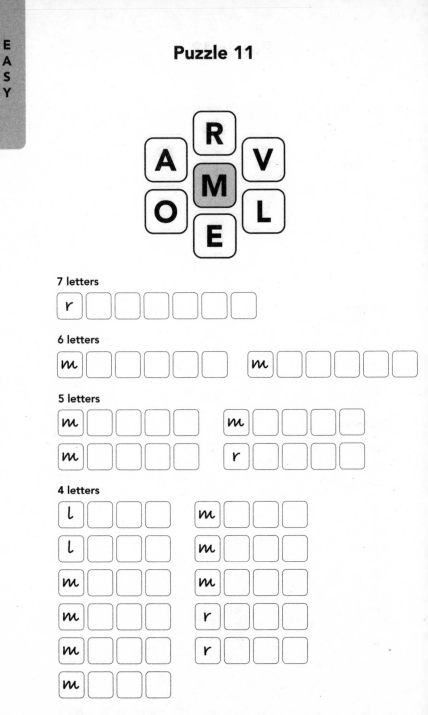

7 letters

r ☐ ☐ ☐ ☐ ☐ ☐

6 letters

m ☐ ☐ ☐ ☐ ☐   m ☐ ☐ ☐ ☐ ☐

5 letters

m ☐ ☐ ☐ ☐   m ☐ ☐ ☐ ☐

m ☐ ☐ ☐ ☐   r ☐ ☐ ☐ ☐

4 letters

l ☐ ☐ ☐   m ☐ ☐ ☐

l ☐ ☐ ☐   m ☐ ☐ ☐

m ☐ ☐ ☐   m ☐ ☐ ☐

m ☐ ☐ ☐   r ☐ ☐ ☐

m ☐ ☐ ☐   r ☐ ☐ ☐

m ☐ ☐ ☐

Puzzle 12

7 letters

c _ _ _ _ _ _

6 letters

r _ _ _ _ _

5 letters

c _ d _ _   c _ _ _ _

c _ r _ _   c r _ _ _

c _ _ _ _

4 letters

c _ _ _   c _ _ _

c _ _ _   c _ _ _

c _ _ _   c _ _ _

E
A
S
Y

7 letters

s

5 letters

e

k i

k n

s

4 letters

e

g

i

k   n

k   g

k   g

k n

s   e

s   n

s   n

Puzzle 14

7 letters

r

6 letters

r

5 letters

m | | | | d   m | | | |

4 letters

d | | | m   m | | d |

d | | | m | | r |

m | e | | m | | v |

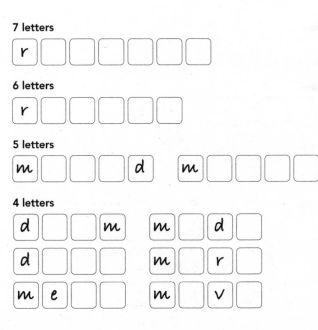

17

Puzzle 15

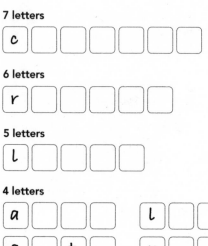

7 letters

c

6 letters

r

5 letters

l

4 letters

a

a t

c

c a

l

r

t

Puzzle 16

7 letters

e ☐ ☐ ☐ ☐ ☐ ☐

6 letters

e ☐ ☐ ☐ ☐ ☐   m ☐ ☐ ☐ ☐ ☐

5 letters

m ☐ l ☐ ☐   m ☐ ☐ ☐ ☐

m ☐ p ☐ ☐   p ☐ ☐ ☐ ☐

4 letters

e ☐ ☐ ☐   m ☐ ☐ s

m ☐ l ☐   p ☐ ☐ ☐

m ☐ ☐ e   s ☐ ☐ ☐

Puzzle 17

7 letters

d □ □ □ □ □ □

6 letters

e □ □ □ □ □

5 letters

e □ □ P □   P □ □ □ □

l □ □ □ □

4 letters

d □ □ P   P □ □ d

d □ P □   P □ o □

l □ P □   P □ l □

P □ □ l

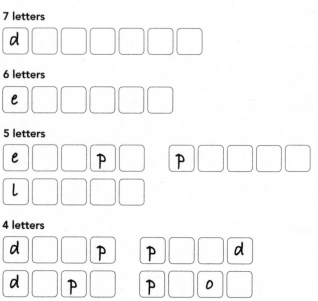

Puzzle 18

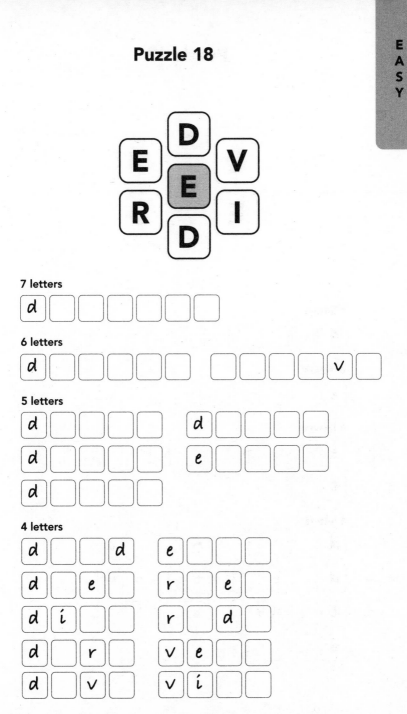

7 letters

d

6 letters

d   v

5 letters

d   d

d   e

d

4 letters

d   d   e

d e   r   e

d i   r   d

d   r   v e

d   v   v i

Puzzle 19

7 letters

e

6 letters

i

5 letters

i   t

n

4 letters

d n   n

d   t   d

n   d   t

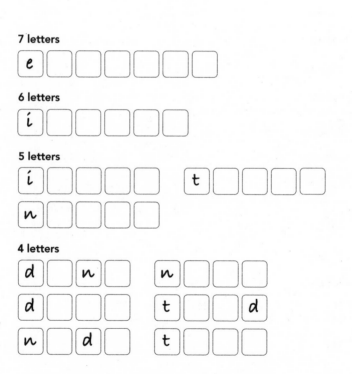

Puzzle 20

7 letters

b □ □ □ □ □ □

6 letters

b □ □ □ □ □   t □ □ □ □ □

5 letters

b o □ □ □   r □ □ □ □

g □ □ □ □   t □ □ □ □

o □ □ □ □

4 letters

b □ □ □   h □ □ □

g □ □ t   r □ □ □

g □ □ □   t □ u □

h □ u □   t □ □ □

Puzzle 21

7 letters

d ☐ ☐ ☐ ☐ ☐ ☐

6 letters

d ☐ ☐ ☐ ☐ ☐

5 letters

d ☐ ☐ ☐ ☐   s ☐ ☐ n ☐

s ☐ ☐ e ☐

4 letters

d ☐ ☐ ☐   s ☐ ☐ p

p ☐ ☐ ☐   s ☐ ☐ ☐

Puzzle 22

7 letters

c						

6 letters

o					

5 letters

c				

s		e		

c				

s				

o				

4 letters

c	e		

c		t	

c			e

o			

c			s

s	c		

c		s	

s		c	

25

7 letters

f

6 letters

f _ _ _ _ e   f _ _ _ _ _

5 letters

f _ _ _ _   u _ _ _ _

4 letters

d _ _ _   f u _ _

d u _ _   n _ _ _

f _ n _   n u _ _

f _ u _   u _ _ _

f o _ _

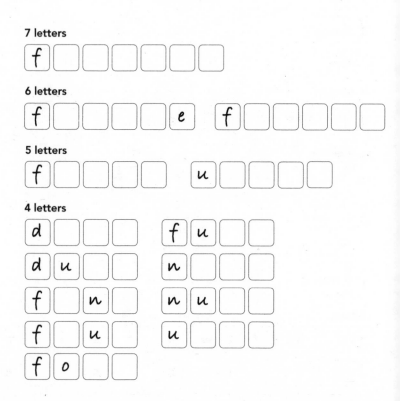

Puzzle 24

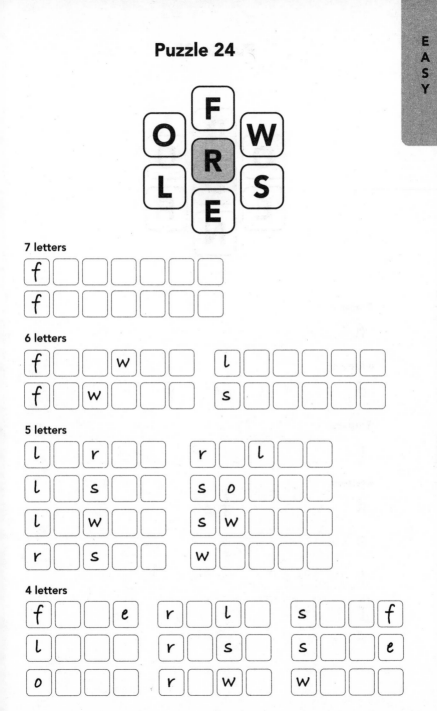

7 letters

f _ _ _ _ _ _

f _ _ _ _ _

6 letters

f _ _ w _ _   l _ _ _ _ _

f _ w _ _ _   s _ _ _ _ _

5 letters

l _ r _ _   r _ _ l _

l _ s _ _   s o _ _ _

l _ w _ _   s w _ _ _

r _ s _ _   w _ _ _ _

4 letters

f _ _ e   r _ l _   s _ _ f

l _ _ _   r _ s _   s _ _ e

o _ _ _   r _ w _   w _ _ _

27

Puzzle 25

7 letters

| h | | | | | | |

6 letters

| d | | | | | |

5 letters

| d | i | | | | | d | | i | | |

4 letters

| d | | | | | h | i | | |

| d | o | | | | h | o | | |

| g | i | | | | i | | | |

| g | o | | | | l | | | |

Puzzle 26

7 letters

g

6 letters

g

r

5 letters

g

g

o

g

i

w

i

g

w

w

o

4 letters

g

n

g

w

g

w

r

g

i

w

g

r

g

Puzzle 27

7 letters

a ⬚ ⬚ ⬚ ⬚ ⬚ ⬚

5 letters

l ⬚ ⬚ ⬚ ⬚   t ⬚ ⬚ ⬚ ⬚

4 letters

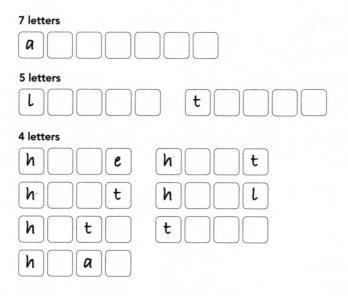

h ⬚ ⬚ e   h ⬚ ⬚ t

h ⬚ ⬚ t   h ⬚ ⬚ l

h ⬚ t ⬚   t ⬚ ⬚ ⬚

h ⬚ a ⬚

Puzzle 28

7 letters

c ◻ ◻ ◻ ◻ ◻ ◻

6 letters

l ◻ ◻ ◻ ◻ ◻   s ◻ ◻ ◻ ◻ ◻

5 letters

c ◻ ◻ ◻ ◻   s ◻ ◻ ◻ ◻

l ◻ ◻ ◻ ◻   s ◻ ◻ ◻ ◻

s ◻ ◻ ◻ ◻

4 letters

a ◻ ◻ ◻   l e ◻ ◻

l ◻ c ◻   s ◻ l ◻

l a ◻ ◻   s ◻ ◻ l

l ◻ a ◻

Puzzle 29

7 letters

t

6 letters

t

5 letters

d   t

d   t

r

4 letters

d   e   d   r   r   d

d r   d e   r e

d t   d r

Puzzle 30

7 letters

c

6 letters

c _ r _ _ _   v _ _ _ _ _

c _ _ _ r _

5 letters

c _ _ _ n   c _ _ _ e

c _ _ _ r   r _ _ _ _

c _ _ _ t

4 letters

c _ _ t   c _ _ n

c _ n _   c _ v _

c _ r _   o _ _ _

E
A
S
Y

7 letters

P [ ] [ ] [ ] [ ] [ ] [ ]

6 letters

P [ ] n [ ] [ ] [ ]   P [ ] [ ] n [ ] [ ]

5 letters

P [ ] l [ ] [ ]   P e [ ] [ ] [ ]

P [ ] [ ] e [ ]   P [ ] [ ] [ ] e

P [ ] d [ ] [ ]   P [ ] [ ] [ ] d

4 letters

l [ ] [ ] [ ]   P [ ] [ ] l

n [ ] [ ] e   P [ ] [ ] n

P [ ] l [ ]   P [ ] [ ] a

P [ ] n [ ]   P [ ] [ ] d

Puzzle 32

7 letters

m

6 letters

m

4 letters

i

m

o | | | t

o | | | o

r i

r o

t | r

t | | m

t | | o

Puzzle 33

7 letters

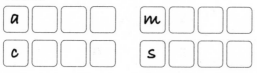

m ☐ ☐ ☐ ☐ ☐ ☐

6 letters

c ☐ ☐ ☐ ☐ ☐

5 letters

c ☐ ☐ ☐ ☐   m ☐ ☐ ☐ ☐

m ☐ ☐ ☐ ☐

4 letters

a ☐ ☐ ☐   m ☐ ☐ ☐

c ☐ ☐ ☐   s ☐ ☐ ☐

Puzzle 34

EASY

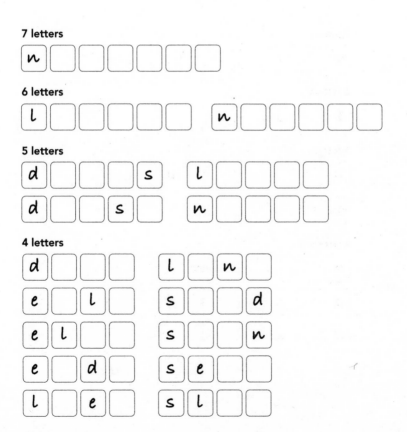

7 letters

n _ _ _ _ _ _

6 letters

l _ _ _ _ _   n _ _ _ _ _

5 letters

d _ _ _ s   l _ _ _ _

d _ _ s _   n _ _ _ _

4 letters

d _ _ _   l _ n _

e _ l _   s _ _ d

e l _ _   s _ _ n

e _ d _   s e _ _

l _ e _   s l _ _

37

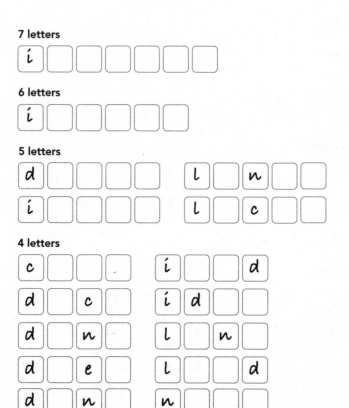

7 letters

i

6 letters

i

5 letters

d   *l* *n*

i   *l* *c*

4 letters

c   *i*   *d*

d *c*   *i* *d*

d *n*   *l* *n*

d *e*   *l*   *d*

d *n*   *n*

Puzzle 36

7 letters

i _ _ _ _ _ _

6 letters

n _ _ _ _ _   t _ _ _ _ _

s _ _ _ _ _

5 letters

n _ _ _ _   t _ _ _ g

s _ _ _ t   t _ _ g _

s _ _ _ g

4 letters

g _ _ s   s _ _ n

g _ s _   s _ _ g

n _ _ _   t _ _ _

s _ _ h

E
A
S
Y

7 letters

S

6 letters

S

5 letters

a

o

n

4 letters

a

o

e

s

n

Puzzle 38

7 letters

c □ □ □ □ □ □

6 letters

i □ □ □ □ □

5 letters

m □ □ □ □

4 letters

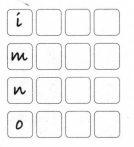

c □ □ n   i □ □ □

c □ m □   m □ □ □

c □ m □   n □ □ □

c □ n □   o □ □ □

41

E
A
S
Y

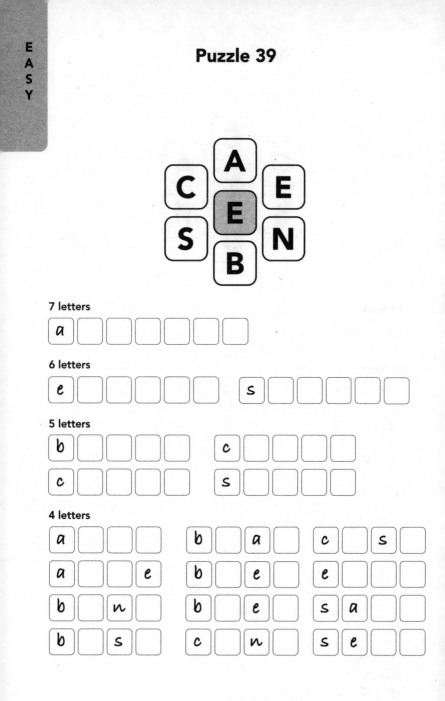

7 letters

a

6 letters

e   s

5 letters

b   c

c   s

4 letters

a   b   a   c   s

a   e   b   e   e

b   n   b   e   s a

b   s   c   n   s e

Puzzle 40

7 letters

| a | | | | | | |

5 letters

| a | | e | | | | d | o | | | |

| a | | o | | | | o | | | | |

| d | a | | | | | t | | | | |

| d | e | | | |

4 letters

| a | | | | | p | o | | |

| d | a | | | | t | | p | |

| d | o | | | | t | | a | |

| p | a | | | | t | | e | |

| p | e | | |

43

7 letters

b

6 letters

b ☐ w ☐ ☐ ☐   r ☐ ☐ ☐ ☐ ☐

b ☐ ☐ w ☐ ☐

5 letters

b ☐ w ☐ ☐   r ☐ w ☐ ☐

b ☐ e ☐ ☐   s ☐ w ☐ ☐

b ☐ o ☐ ☐   s w ☐ ☐ ☐

r ☐ ☐ ☐ w   w ☐ ☐ ☐ ☐

4 letters

b ☐ w ☐   o ☐ ☐ ☐   w e ☐ ☐

b ☐ ☐ w   o ☐ ☐ s   w ☐ ☐ e

b ☐ o ☐   r ☐ ☐ ☐   w ☐ ☐ e

Puzzle 42

7 letters

a ☐☐☐☐☐☐

6 letters

g ☐☐☐☐☐   r ☐☐☐☐☐

5 letters

a ☐☐☐☐   r ☐☐☐☐

g ☐☐☐☐   v ☐☐☐☐

4 letters

a ☐☐☐   r ☐☐☐

e ☐☐☐   v ☐☐☐

g ☐☐☐

7 letters

e _ _ _ _ _ _

q _ _ _ _ _ _

6 letters

r _ _ _ _ _   s _ _ _ _ _

5 letters

r _ _ _ _

4 letters

r i _ _   s i _ _

r _ _ s   s u _ _

r u _ _   s _ _ _

s e _ _   u _ _ _

Puzzle 44

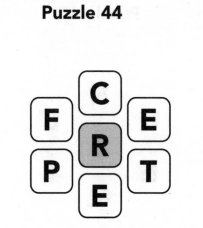

7 letters

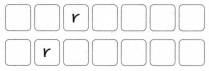

5 letters

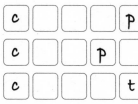

4 letters

7 letters

u ☐ ☐ ☐ ☐ ☐ ☐

5 letters

f ☐ e ☐ ☐   i ☐ ☐ u ☐

f ☐ n ☐ ☐   u ☐ ☐ ☐ ☐

i ☐ ☐ i ☐

4 letters

d i ☐ ☐   f ☐ u ☐

d u ☐ ☐   f ☐ ☐ e

f e ☐ ☐   n ☐ ☐ ☐

Puzzle 46

7 letters

| v | | | | | | |

6 letters

| t | | | | | |

5 letters

| a | | | | | | n | | v | | |

| e | | | | | | r | | v | | |

| n | | | v | |

4 letters

| a | | | | | e | | | r | | v | a | | |

| e | | | | | n | | | | | v | e | | |

| e | | | n | | r | | | | | v | e | | |

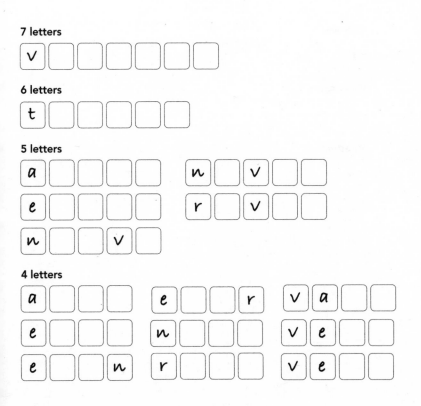

Puzzle 47

7 letters

b

5 letters

b

4 letters

b _ g _   b _ _ e

b _ _ t   b _ _ s

b _ t _

Puzzle 48

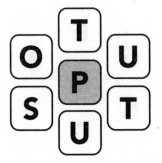

7 letters

O

6 letters

O

5 letters

P _ u _ _   s _ _ _ _

P u _ _ _

4 letters

O _ t _   P _ u _   s _ O _

O _ u _   P _ t _   s t _ _

P _ s _   P _ _ t   t O _ _

P _ t _   s _ u _

Puzzle 49

7 letters

S

6 letters

i

r

5 letters

i

r

r

S

S

u

4 letters

O

S

r

S

S

u

S

u

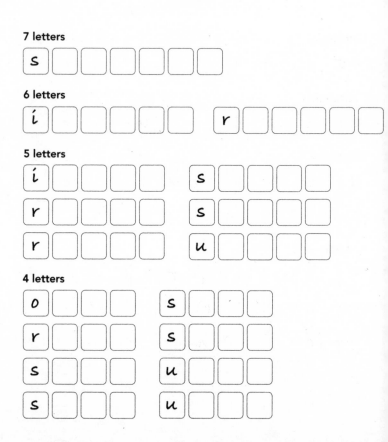

Puzzle 50

7 letters

u ⬚ ⬚ ⬚ ⬚ ⬚ ⬚

6 letters

i ⬚ ⬚ ⬚ ⬚ ⬚   u ⬚ ⬚ ⬚ ⬚ ⬚

5 letters

f ⬚ ⬚ ⬚ ⬚   m ⬚ ⬚ ⬚ ⬚

m ⬚ ⬚ ⬚ ⬚

4 letters

f i ⬚ ⬚   f r ⬚ ⬚

f o ⬚ ⬚   m ⬚ ⬚ ⬚

f o ⬚ ⬚   n ⬚ ⬚ ⬚

Puzzle 51

7 letters

s ☐ ☐ ☐ ☐ ☐ ☐

6 letters

u ☐ ☐ ☐ ☐ ☐

5 letters

g ☐ ☐ ☐ ☐   u ☐ ☐ ☐ ☐

s ☐ ☐ ☐ ☐   u ☐ ☐ ☐ ☐

4 letters

g ☐ ☐ y   r ☐ ☐ ☐

g ☐ y ☐   u ☐ ☐ ☐

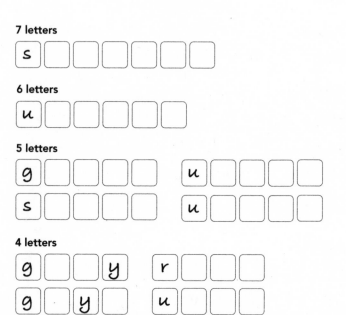

Puzzle 52

7 letters

P

6 letters

r

5 letters

e   t

e   t

n   v

n   v

p

t

4 letters

e

e   r

p

r

t   n

t   r

t   e

v   r

v   t

Puzzle 53

7 letters

t

6 letters

t

5 letters

g

g

i

t

4 letters

g | l

g | l

g | t

t

Puzzle 54

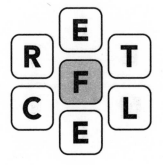

7 letters

r ▢ ▢ ▢ ▢ ▢ ▢

6 letters

r ▢ ▢ ▢ ▢ ▢

5 letters

c ▢ ▢ ▢ ▢   f ▢ ▢ ▢ t

4 letters

c ▢ ▢ ▢   f l ▢ ▢

f ▢ ▢ l   f r ▢ ▢

f ▢ ▢ t   f r ▢ ▢

f ▢ l ▢   l ▢ ▢ ▢

f ▢ t ▢   r ▢ ▢ ▢

7 letters

c _ _ _ _ _ _

6 letters

c _ n _ _ _   c _ _ n _ _

5 letters

c _ _ _ _   s _ _ _ _

4 letters

c _ _ _   s _ _ n

n _ u _   t o _ _

n _ t _   t u _ _

o _ _ _   u _ _ _

s _ _ t

Puzzle 56

7 letters

a

6 letters

a

5 letters

a   n   t

n   s   s   n

n   t   s   n

4 letters

a   t

a

7 letters

a

6 letters

l

5 letters

a   p

i   p

p   p

4 letters

a   l   p

d   l   p

i   p   p

i   p

Puzzle 58

7 letters

O						

6 letters

P					

5 letters

O				

4 letters

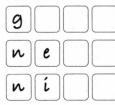

g			

n	e		

n	i		

n	o		

o			

p			

Puzzle 59

7 letters

| o | | | | | | |

6 letters

| o | | | | | |

5 letters

| c | | | | | | s | | | | |

| f | | | | |

4 letters

| c | | | | | f | | | i |

| f | | | e | | f | | | s |

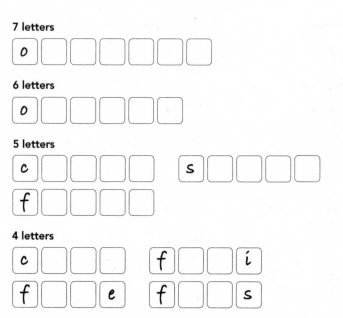

Puzzle 60

7 letters

m						

4 letters

e			

i			

m			n

m		n	

m			t

m		t	

m	o		

o		e	

o			t

t	i		

t	o		

Puzzle 61

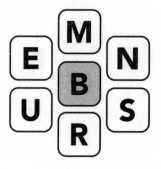

7 letters

n ⬜ ⬜ ⬜ ⬜ ⬜ ⬜

6 letters

n ⬜ ⬜ ⬜ ⬜ ⬜

5 letters

b e ⬜ ⬜ ⬜   n ⬜ ⬜ ⬜ ⬜

b u ⬜ ⬜ ⬜   u ⬜ ⬜ ⬜ ⬜

4 letters

b ⬜ ⬜ m   n ⬜ b ⬜

b ⬜ m ⬜   n ⬜ m ⬜

b ⬜ n ⬜   r ⬜ ⬜ ⬜

b ⬜ ⬜ n   s ⬜ ⬜ ⬜

Puzzle 62

7 letters

o						

6 letters

g					

o					

5 letters

g		o		

i				

4 letters

i	o		

s		o	

i		o	

s	o		

n			

Puzzle 63

7 letters

c □ □ □ □ □ □

6 letters

c □ □ □ □ □   g □ □ □ □ □

5 letters

c □ g □ □   g □ □ □ e

c □ □ g □   r □ □ □ □

g □ □ □ s

4 letters

a □ □ □   h □ □ □

c □ g □   r □ □ e

c □ □ g   r □ □ s

g □ □ h   s □ g □

g □ □ r   s □ □ g

Puzzle 64

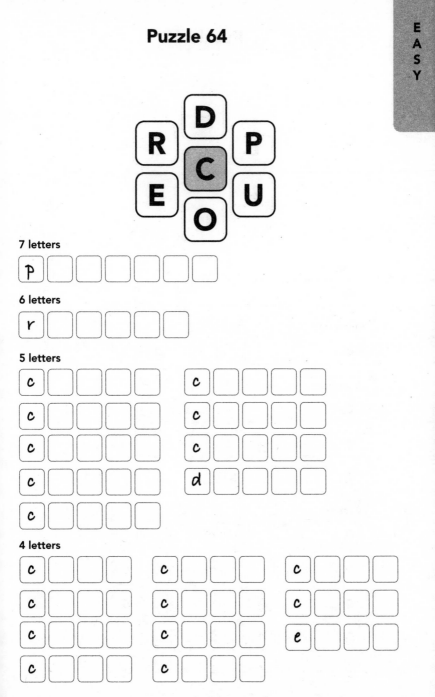

7 letters

P

6 letters

r

5 letters

c

c

c

c

c

c

c

c

d

4 letters

c

c

c

c

c

c

c

c

c

c

e

Puzzle 65

7 letters

c

6 letters

e   f

5 letters

f   r   f   l

f   r   f l

4 letters

c   e   f   r   f u

c   l   f   r   f u

c l   f l   l

f   c   f l

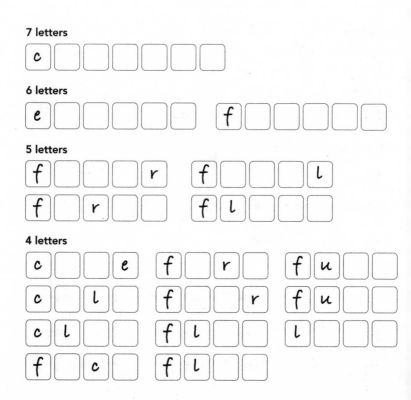

Puzzle 66

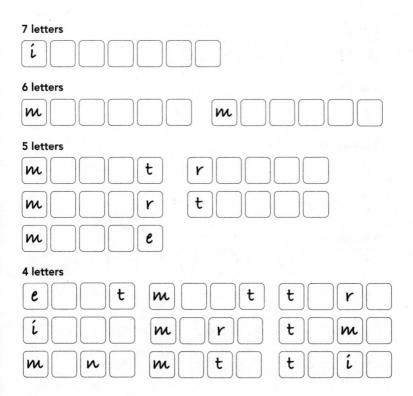

7 letters

i

6 letters

m   m

5 letters

m _ _ _ t   r _ _ _ _

m _ _ _ r   t _ _ _ _

m _ _ _ e

4 letters

e _ _ t   m _ _ t   t _ r _

i _ _ _   m _ r _   t _ m _

m _ n _   m _ t _   t _ i _

69

7 letters

w ☐ ☐ ☐ ☐ ☐ ☐

6 letters

w ☐ k ☐ ☐ ☐   w ☐ l ☐ ☐ ☐

5 letters

a ☐ ☐ ☐ n   a ☐ ☐ n ☐

4 letters

a ☐ ☐ ☐   l ☐ ☐ k

g ☐ ☐ ☐   n ☐ ☐ ☐

k ☐ ☐ n   w ☐ ☐ l

k ☐ ☐ g   w ☐ ☐ g

l ☐ ☐ n   w ☐ ☐ k

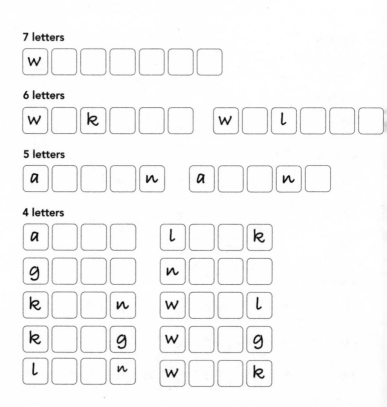

Puzzle 68

7 letters

c

6 letters

c

5 letters

a

c a

c s

c a

c s

c c

4 letters

a e

c h

a h

e h

c e

e h

71

Puzzle 69

7 letters

P □ □ □ □ □ □

6 letters

P □ L □ □ □   P L □ □ □ □

P □ Y □ □ □

5 letters

a □ □ □ g   P □ □ □ n

4 letters

P □ □ L   P □ □ g

P □ □ n   P □ □ n

P □ □ g   P □ □ y

Puzzle 70

7 letters

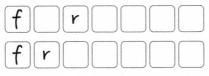

6 letters

5 letters

4 letters

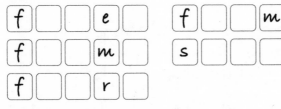

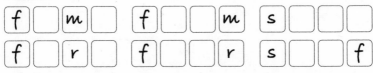

E
A
S
Y

7 letters

w

6 letters

r

5 letters

g

w　　i

o

w　　o

4 letters

g　　　n

w　　　k

g　　　w

w　　　k

k

w　　　n

w　　　g

Puzzle 72

7 letters

P □ □ □ □ □ □

6 letters

P □ □ □ □ □

5 letters

P □ □ □ □

4 letters

f □ i □   P □ l □

f □ o □   P □ r □

l □ □ □   r □ □ e

P □ □ r   r □ □ e

P □ l □

7 letters

g

6 letters

d

5 letters

d

d

d

4 letters

d _ e _

d _ g _

d _ s _

e _ _ _

g _ d _

g _ e _

o _ d _

o _ e _

s _ _ _

Puzzle 74

7 letters

u _ _ _ _ _ _

6 letters

u _ _ _ _ _

5 letters

d _ _ _ _   w _ _ p _

w _ _ d _   w _ _ p _

4 letters

d _ _ _   w _ _ p

p _ _ _   w _ _ s

s _ _ _   w _ _ p

w _ _ s   w _ _ p

w _ _ d

Puzzle 75

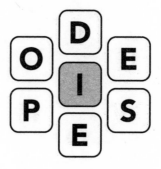

7 letters

e

6 letters

e

p

5 letters

p

s

4 letters

d _ e _

p _ _ d

d _ p _

p _ _ s

i _ _ _

s _ _ _

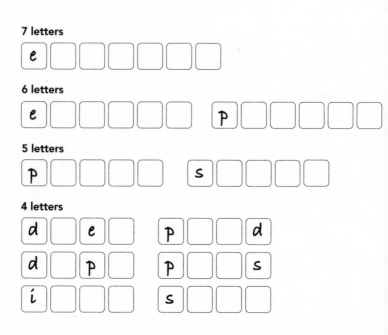

Puzzle 76

7 letters

g

6 letters

l   o

5 letters

g   l

l   o

4 letters

g   w   l

g   g   w

g   n

7 letters

c · · · · · ·

6 letters

p · · · · ·

5 letters

a · · · ·   c · · l ·

c · · · l   p · · · ·

4 letters

c · p ·   l · · ·

c · · p   p · · e

Puzzle 78

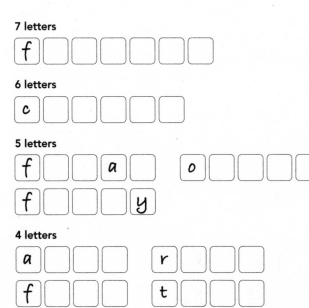

7 letters

f _ _ _ _ _ _

6 letters

c _ _ _ _ _

5 letters

f _ _ a _   o _ _ _ _

f _ _ _ y

4 letters

a _ _ _   r _ _ _

f _ _ _   t _ _ _

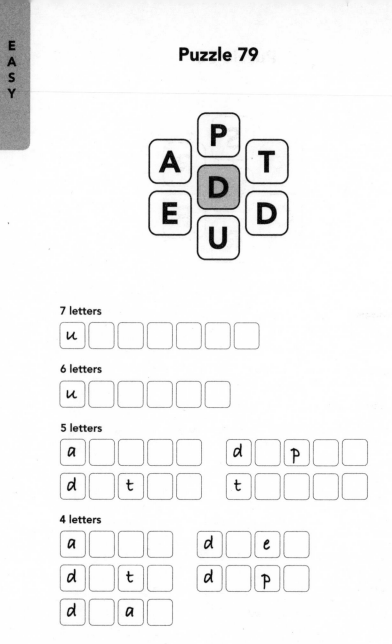

7 letters

u

6 letters

u

5 letters

a

d   p

d   t

t

4 letters

a

d   e

d   t

d   p

d   a

Puzzle 80

7 letters

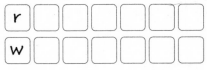

r ▢ ▢ ▢ ▢ ▢ ▢

w ▢ ▢ ▢ ▢ ▢ ▢

6 letters

r ▢ ▢ ▢ ▢ ▢   w ▢ ▢ ▢ ▢ ▢

5 letters

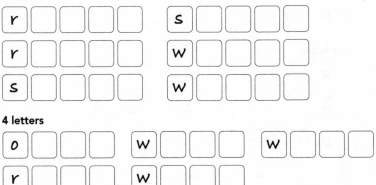

r ▢ ▢ ▢ ▢   s ▢ ▢ ▢ ▢

r ▢ ▢ ▢ ▢   w ▢ ▢ ▢ ▢

s ▢ ▢ ▢ ▢   w ▢ ▢ ▢ ▢

4 letters

o ▢ ▢ ▢   w ▢ ▢ ▢   w ▢ ▢ ▢

r ▢ ▢ ▢   w ▢ ▢

s ▢ ▢ ▢   w ▢ ▢

Puzzle 81

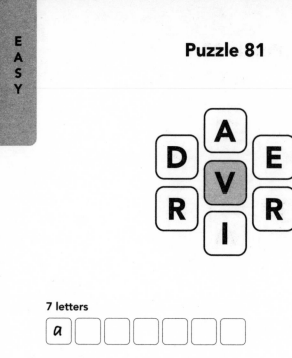

7 letters

a ☐ ☐ ☐ ☐ ☐ ☐

6 letters

a ☐ ☐ ☐ ☐ ☐   v ☐ ☐ ☐ ☐ ☐

d ☐ ☐ ☐ ☐ ☐

5 letters

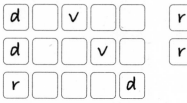

d ☐ v ☐ ☐   r ☐ ☐ ☐ r

d ☐ ☐ v ☐   r ☐ ☐ ☐ r

r ☐ ☐ ☐ d

4 letters

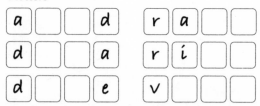

a ☐ ☐ d   r a ☐ ☐

d ☐ ☐ a   r i ☐ ☐

d ☐ ☐ e   v ☐ ☐ ☐

Puzzle 82

7 letters

P						

5 letters

e				

P				

4 letters

n		P	

P			t

P			e

t			P

P			t

t		P	

P			e

t		P	

P			t

7 letters

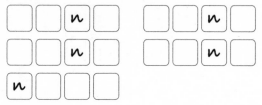

5 letters

4 letters

Puzzle 84

7 letters

☐ ☐ ☐ *i* ☐ ☐ ☐

5 letters

☐ ☐ ☐ *i* ☐   ☐ ☐ ☐ *i* ☐

4 letters

☐ *i* ☐ ☐   ☐ *i* ☐ ☐

☐ ☐ *i* ☐   ☐ ☐ *i* ☐

Puzzle 85

7 letters

6 letters

4 letters

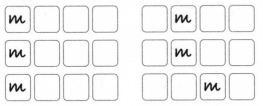

Puzzle 86

MEDIUM

7 letters

5 letters

4 letters

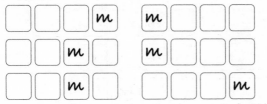

Puzzle 87

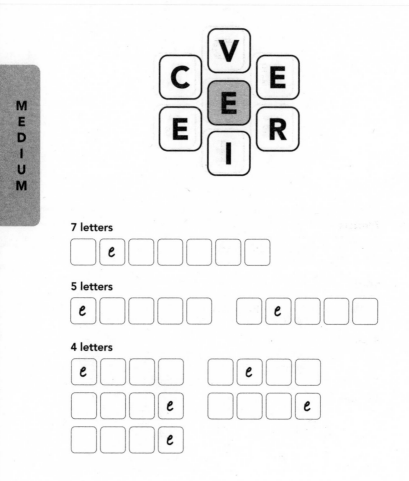

7 letters

5 letters

4 letters

7 letters

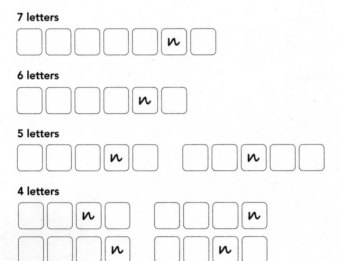

6 letters

5 letters

4 letters

MEDIUM

Puzzle 89

MEDIUM

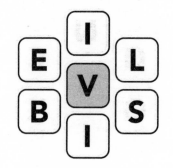

7 letters

V ☐ ☐ ☐ ☐ ☐ ☐

5 letters

☐ V ☐ ☐ ☐   V ☐ ☐ ☐ ☐

☐ ☐ V ☐ ☐

4 letters

☐ V ☐ ☐   V ☐ ☐ ☐

☐ ☐ V ☐   V ☐ ☐ ☐

V ☐ ☐ ☐

Puzzle 90

7 letters

◻ O ◻ ◻ ◻ ◻ ◻

6 letters

◻ O ◻ ◻ ◻ ◻   ◻ O ◻ ◻ ◻ ◻

4 letters

◻ O ◻ ◻   ◻ O ◻ ◻

◻ O ◻ ◻   ◻ O ◻ ◻

◻ ◻ O ◻

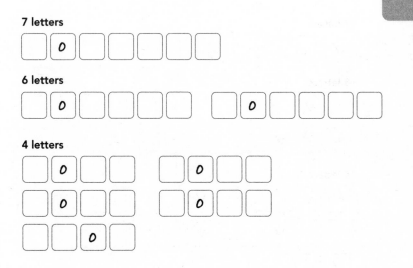

Puzzle 91

7 letters

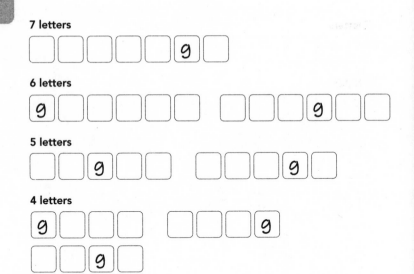

6 letters

5 letters

4 letters

7 letters

f □ □ □ □ □ □

5 letters

f □ □ □ □   f □ □ □ □

f □ □ □ □

4 letters

f □ □ □   f □ □ □

f □ □ □   f □ □ □

f □ □ □

7 letters

		O				

5 letters

	O			

	O			

4 letters

	O		

O			

	O		

O			

	O		

Puzzle 94

7 letters

⬜⬜⬜⬜⬜⬜*m*

6 letters

⬜⬜⬜⬜⬜*m*   *m*⬜⬜⬜⬜⬜

5 letters

m⬜⬜⬜⬜

4 letters

⬜⬜⬜*m*   *m*⬜⬜⬜

⬜⬜⬜*m*   ⬜⬜⬜*m*

⬜⬜⬜*m*

MEDIUM

7 letters

⬜⬜⬜⬜⬜ W ⬜

6 letters

⬜⬜⬜⬜⬜ W

5 letters

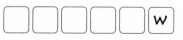

⬜⬜⬜ W ⬜   W ⬜⬜⬜⬜

⬜⬜ W ⬜⬜

4 letters

⬜⬜⬜ W   W ⬜⬜⬜

⬜⬜ W ⬜   W ⬜⬜⬜

Puzzle 96

7 letters

f _ _ _ _ _ _

5 letters

f _ _ _ _   f _ _ _ _

4 letters

f _ _ _   f _ _ _

f _ _ _   f _ _ _

f _ _ _   f _ _ _

Puzzle 97

7 letters

6 letters

4 letters

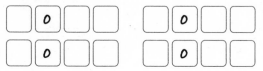

Puzzle 98

7 letters

| V | | | | | | |

6 letters

| | | V | | | |

5 letters

| | | V | | | | | | V | | | |

| | | | V | | | | | V | | |

4 letters

| | | V | | | V | | | |

| | | V | | | V | | | |

MEDIUM

7 letters

6 letters

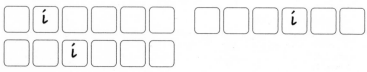

5 letters

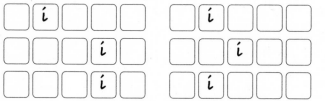

4 letters

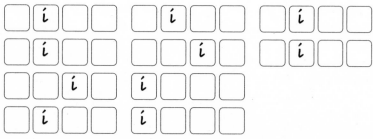

Puzzle 100

7 letters

6 letters

5 letters

4 letters

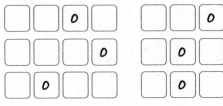

Puzzle 101

7 letters

6 letters

5 letters

4 letters

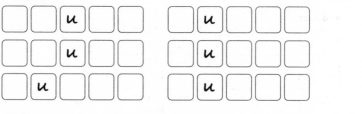

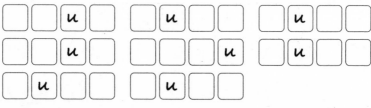

Puzzle 102

MEDIUM

7 letters

6 letters

5 letters

4 letters

 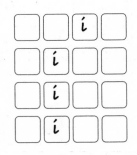

Puzzle 103

MEDIUM

7 letters

☐☐☐ C ☐☐☐

5 letters

☐ C ☐☐☐ ☐☐☐☐☐ (C ☐☐☐☐)

☐☐☐ C ☐ C ☐☐☐☐

☐☐☐ C ☐

4 letters

☐ C ☐☐ C ☐☐☐

☐ C ☐☐ ☐☐ C ☐

C ☐☐☐ ☐ C ☐☐

C ☐☐☐

106

Puzzle 104

7 letters

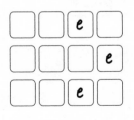

5 letters

4 letters

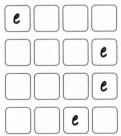

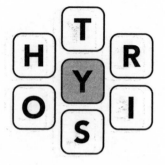

7 letters

⬜⬜⬜⬜⬜⬜ y

6 letters

⬜⬜⬜⬜⬜ y

5 letters

⬜⬜⬜⬜ y   ⬜⬜⬜⬜ y

4 letters

⬜⬜ y ⬜   ⬜⬜ y ⬜

⬜⬜⬜ y

Puzzle 106

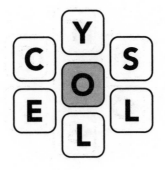

7 letters

⬜ ⬜ O ⬜ ⬜ ⬜ ⬜

6 letters

⬜ ⬜ ⬜ ⬜ O ⬜   ⬜ O ⬜ ⬜ ⬜ ⬜

5 letters

⬜ ⬜ ⬜ ⬜ O   ⬜ ⬜ ⬜ O ⬜

4 letters

⬜ ⬜ O ⬜   ⬜ O ⬜ ⬜

⬜ O ⬜ ⬜   ⬜ ⬜ O ⬜

⬜ O ⬜ ⬜   ⬜ O ⬜ ⬜

Puzzle 107

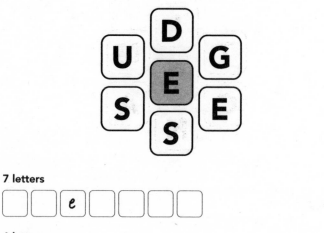

7 letters

6 letters

5 letters

4 letters

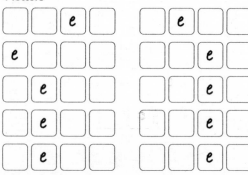

Puzzle 108

7 letters

c □ □ □ □ □ □

6 letters

□ c □ □ □ □   c □ □ □ □ □

□ □ □ □ □ c   □ □ c □ □ □

c □ □ □ □ □   □ □ □ □ □ c

5 letters

□ □ □ □ c   c □ □ □ □

c □ □ □ □   □ □ □ □ c

4 letters

c □ □ □   □ c □ □

c □ □ □   □ □ c □

c □ □ □

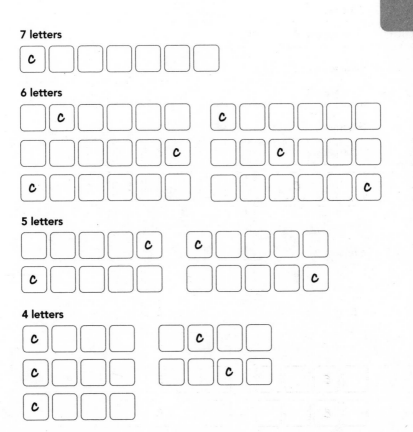

111

7 letters

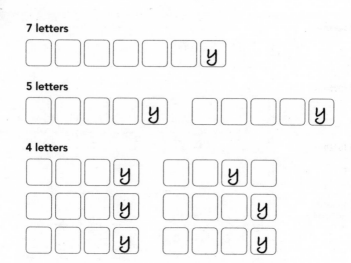

5 letters

4 letters

Puzzle 110

7 letters

6 letters

5 letters

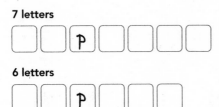

4 letters

Puzzle 111

7 letters

m ⬜ ⬜ ⬜ ⬜ ⬜ ⬜

6 letters

⬜ ⬜ ⬜ ⬜ *m* ⬜   ⬜ ⬜ *m* ⬜ ⬜ ⬜

5 letters

⬜ ⬜ *m* ⬜ ⬜   *m* ⬜ ⬜ ⬜ ⬜

⬜ *m* ⬜ ⬜ ⬜

4 letters

⬜ *m* ⬜ ⬜   *m* ⬜ ⬜ ⬜

⬜ ⬜ *m* ⬜   *m* ⬜ ⬜ ⬜

m ⬜ ⬜ ⬜   *m* ⬜ ⬜ ⬜

m ⬜ ⬜ ⬜   ⬜ ⬜ *m* ⬜

Puzzle 112

7 letters

☐☐☐☐☐ f ☐

6 letters

☐☐☐☐☐ f

5 letters

f ☐☐☐☐   f ☐☐☐☐

f ☐☐☐☐   f ☐☐☐☐

4 letters

☐☐☐ f   f ☐☐☐

f ☐☐☐   f ☐☐☐

f ☐☐☐   ☐☐ f ☐

f ☐☐☐   ☐☐☐ f

Puzzle 113

MEDIUM

7 letters

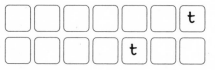

5 letters

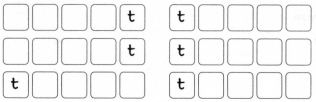

4 letters

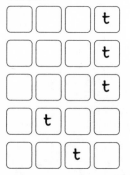
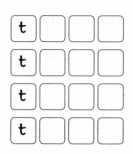

Puzzle 114

7 letters

m □ □ □ □ □ □

6 letters

m □ □ □ □ □   m □ □ □ □ □

5 letters

m □ □ □ □   □ □ □ m □

m □ □ □ □   □ □ □ m □

4 letters

□ □ m □   m □ □ □

□ m □ □   □ □ □ m

m □ □ □   □ □ □ m

m □ □ □   □ □ m □

m □ □ □

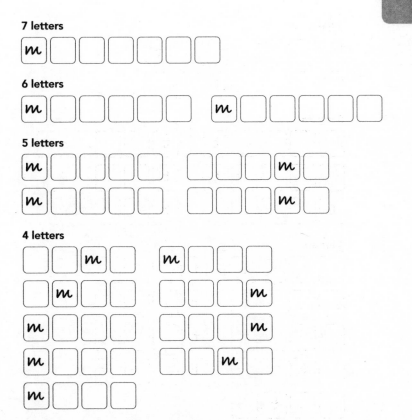

Puzzle 115

7 letters

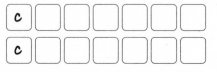

6 letters

5 letters

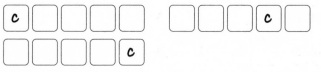

4 letters

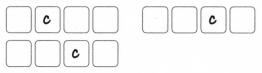

Puzzle 116

7 letters

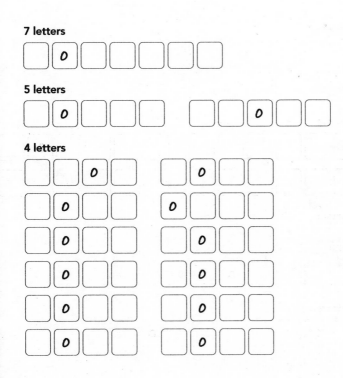

5 letters

4 letters

Puzzle 117

7 letters

6 letters

5 letters

4 letters

7 letters

☐☐☐☐*i*☐☐

☐☐☐☐*i*☐☐

6 letters

☐☐☐*i*☐☐

5 letters

☐☐☐*i*☐ ☐☐☐*i*☐

☐☐*i*☐☐ ☐*i*☐☐☐

☐☐*i*☐☐

4 letters

☐*i*☐☐ ☐*i*☐☐

☐*i*☐☐ ☐*i*☐☐

MEDIUM

7 letters

☐ ☐ f ☐ ☐ ☐ ☐

6 letters

f ☐ ☐ ☐ ☐ ☐   ☐ ☐ f ☐ ☐ ☐

5 letters

f ☐ ☐ ☐ ☐

4 letters

f ☐ ☐ ☐   f ☐ ☐ ☐

f ☐ ☐ ☐   f ☐ ☐ ☐

f ☐ ☐ ☐   ☐ ☐ f ☐

f ☐ ☐ ☐

Puzzle 120

7 letters

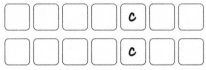

6 letters

5 letters

4 letters

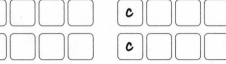

Puzzle 121

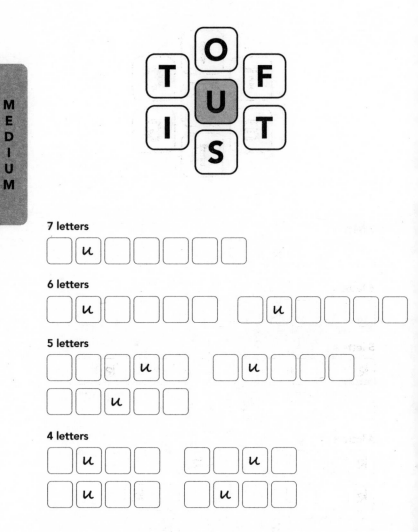

7 letters

6 letters

5 letters

4 letters

Puzzle 122

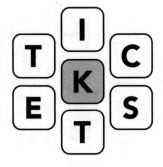

7 letters

6 letters

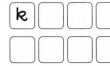

5 letters

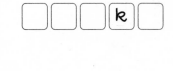

4 letters

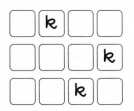

Puzzle 123

7 letters

☐☐☐ V ☐☐☐

6 letters

☐☐ V ☐☐☐   ☐☐☐ V ☐☐

☐☐☐ V ☐☐   ☐☐☐ V ☐☐

5 letters

☐☐ V ☐☐   ☐☐☐ V ☐

☐☐ V ☐☐   ☐☐ V ☐☐

4 letters

☐☐ V ☐   V ☐☐☐

☐☐ V ☐   V ☐☐☐

Puzzle 124

7 letters

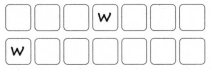

6 letters

5 letters

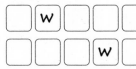

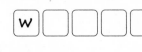

4 letters

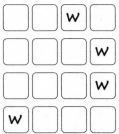

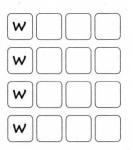

Puzzle 125

7 letters

⬜ ⬜ *c* ⬜ ⬜ ⬜ ⬜

6 letters

c ⬜ ⬜ ⬜ ⬜ ⬜

5 letters

⬜ ⬜ ⬜ ⬜ *c*　⬜ ⬜ ⬜ *c* ⬜

4 letters

⬜ *c* ⬜ ⬜　*c* ⬜ ⬜ ⬜

c ⬜ ⬜ ⬜　*c* ⬜ *t* ⬜

c ⬜ ⬜ ⬜　⬜ ⬜ *c* ⬜

Puzzle 126

7 letters

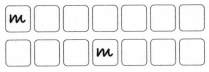

6 letters

4 letters

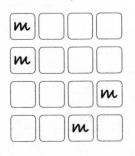

Puzzle 127

7 letters

6 letters

5 letters

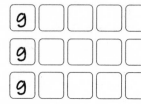 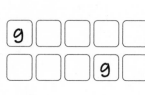

4 letters

Puzzle 128

7 letters

☐ ☐ ☐ ☐ **b** ☐ ☐

6 letters

b ☐ ☐ ☐ ☐ ☐

5 letters

b ☐ ☐ ☐ ☐   ☐ ☐ **b** ☐ ☐

b ☐ ☐ ☐ ☐

4 letters

☐ **b** ☐ ☐   **b** ☐ ☐ ☐

b ☐ ☐ ☐   **b** ☐ ☐ ☐

b ☐ ☐ ☐

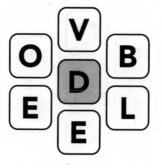

7 letters

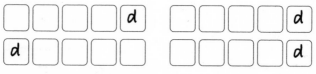

5 letters

4 letters

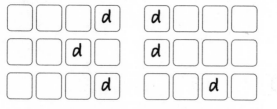

Puzzle 130

7 letters

g ☐ ☐ ☐ ☐ ☐ ☐

6 letters

g ☐ ☐ ☐ ☐ ☐

5 letters

g ☐ ☐ ☐ ☐   g ☐ ☐ ☐ ☐

g ☐ ☐ ☐ ☐

4 letters

☐ ☐ g ☐   g ☐ ☐ ☐

☐ ☐ g ☐   g ☐ ☐ ☐

☐ g ☐ ☐   g ☐ ☐ ☐

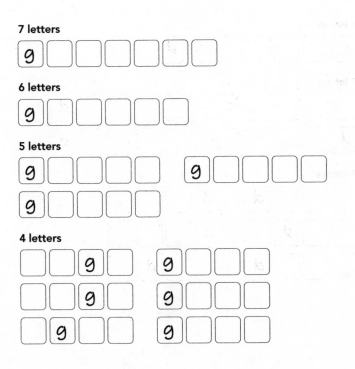

Puzzle 131

7 letters

6 letters

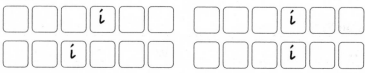

5 letters

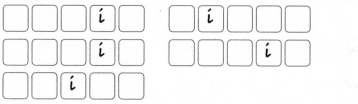

4 letters

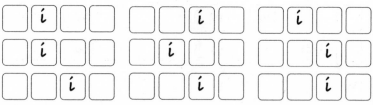

Puzzle 132

7 letters

W ☐ ☐ ☐ ☐ ☐ ☐

W ☐ ☐ ☐ ☐ ☐

6 letters

W ☐ ☐ ☐ ☐ ☐   W ☐ ☐ ☐ ☐ ☐

5 letters

☐ ☐ ☐ ☐ W   W ☐ ☐ ☐ ☐

W ☐ ☐ ☐ ☐   W ☐ ☐ ☐ ☐

W ☐ ☐ ☐ ☐

4 letters

☐ ☐ ☐ W   W ☐ ☐ ☐   W ☐ ☐ ☐

☐ W ☐ ☐   W ☐ ☐ ☐   W ☐ ☐ ☐

W ☐ ☐ ☐   W ☐ ☐ ☐

135

Puzzle 133

7 letters

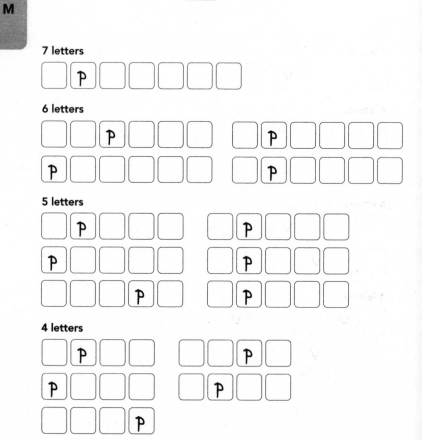

6 letters

5 letters

4 letters

Puzzle 134

7 letters

⬚ ⬚ ⬚ V ⬚ ⬚ ⬚

6 letters

⬚ ⬚ ⬚ V ⬚ ⬚   ⬚ ⬚ V ⬚ ⬚ ⬚

⬚ ⬚ ⬚ V ⬚ ⬚   V ⬚ ⬚ ⬚ ⬚ ⬚

5 letters

⬚ ⬚ ⬚ V ⬚   V ⬚ ⬚ ⬚ ⬚

⬚ ⬚ V ⬚ ⬚   V ⬚ ⬚ ⬚ ⬚

4 letters

⬚ V ⬚ ⬚   V ⬚ ⬚ ⬚

⬚ ⬚ V ⬚

137

Puzzle 135

7 letters

V □ □ □ □ □ □

6 letters

V □ □ □ □ □

5 letters

□ V □ □ □   □ □ V □ □

4 letters

□ □ V □

V □ □ □

V □ □ □

Puzzle 136

7 letters

☐☐☐☐☐☐ y

6 letters

☐☐☐☐☐ y   ☐☐☐☐☐ y

5 letters

☐☐☐☐ y   ☐☐☐☐ y

4 letters

y ☐☐☐   y ☐☐☐

Puzzle 137

MEDIUM

7 letters

⬜⬜⬜⬜ b ⬜⬜

6 letters

b ⬜⬜⬜⬜⬜   ⬜⬜⬜ b ⬜

5 letters

⬜⬜ b ⬜⬜   b ⬜⬜⬜⬜

b ⬜⬜⬜⬜   b ⬜⬜⬜⬜

4 letters

b ⬜⬜⬜   b ⬜⬜⬜

b ⬜⬜⬜   ⬜⬜⬜ b

b ⬜⬜⬜   ⬜⬜⬜ b

b ⬜⬜⬜

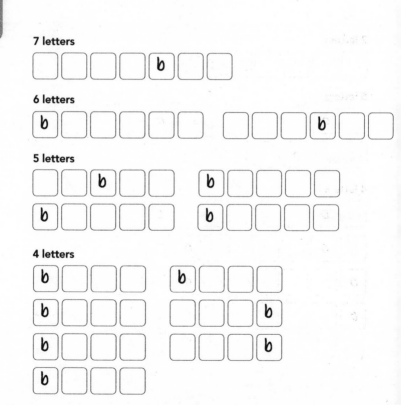

Puzzle 138

7 letters

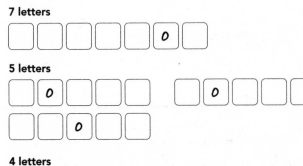

5 letters

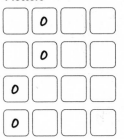

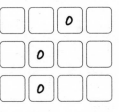

4 letters

Puzzle 139

7 letters

⬜⬜⬜ m ⬜⬜⬜

6 letters

⬜⬜⬜ m ⬜⬜

5 letters

m ⬜⬜⬜⬜   ⬜⬜ m ⬜⬜

4 letters

m ⬜⬜⬜   ⬜⬜⬜ m

m ⬜⬜⬜   ⬜⬜ m ⬜

m ⬜⬜⬜   ⬜⬜⬜ m

m ⬜⬜⬜   ⬜⬜⬜ m

m ⬜⬜⬜   ⬜⬜ m ⬜

⬜⬜⬜ m

Puzzle 140

7 letters

c

6 letters

c   c

c

5 letters

c   c

c   c

c   c

c

4 letters

c   c   c

c   c   c

c   c

143

Puzzle 141

7 letters

5 letters

4 letters

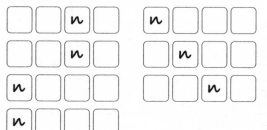

Puzzle 142

7 letters

☐ ☐ r ☐ ☐ ☐ ☐

6 letters

☐ ☐ r ☐ ☐ ☐   r ☐ ☐ ☐ ☐ ☐

☐ ☐ ☐ ☐ r ☐

5 letters

r ☐ ☐ ☐ ☐

4 letters

☐ ☐ r ☐   ☐ ☐ r ☐

☐ ☐ r ☐   ☐ ☐ r ☐

☐ r ☐ ☐   r ☐ ☐ ☐

☐ ☐ r ☐   r ☐ ☐ ☐

Puzzle 143

7 letters

5 letters

4 letters

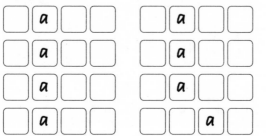

Puzzle 144

7 letters

c _ _ _ _ _ _

6 letters

c _ _ _ _ _   _ _ c _ _ _

5 letters

_ c _ _ _   c _ _ _ _

c _ _ _ _   c _ _ _ _

4 letters

_ c _ _   c _ _ _

_ c _ _   c _ _ _

_ c _ _   c _ _ _

c _ _ _   _ _ c _

c _ _ _   _ c _ _

147

Puzzle 145

7 letters

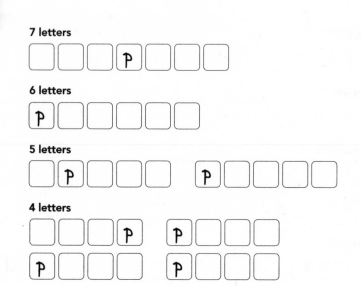

6 letters

5 letters

4 letters

Puzzle 146

7 letters

◻◻◻◻◻d◻

6 letters

◻◻◻◻◻d

5 letters

d◻◻◻◻ ◻◻◻d◻

◻◻◻d◻

4 letters

◻◻d◻ ◻◻d◻ ◻◻◻d

d◻◻◻ ◻◻◻d ◻◻◻d

d◻◻◻ ◻◻◻d ◻◻◻d

d◻◻◻ ◻◻d◻

Puzzle 147

MEDIUM

7 letters

6 letters

5 letters

4 letters

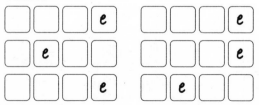

7 letters

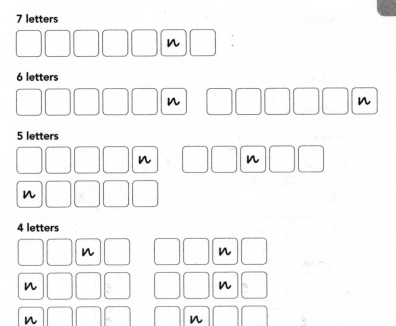

6 letters

5 letters

4 letters

Puzzle 149

7 letters

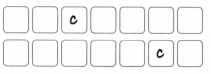

6 letters

5 letters

4 letters

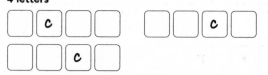

Puzzle 150

7 letters

☐☐☐ r ☐☐☐

6 letters

☐☐ r ☐☐☐

5 letters

☐☐☐☐ r   ☐☐ r ☐☐

☐☐☐ r ☐   ☐ r ☐☐☐

☐☐☐ r ☐   ☐☐☐☐ r

4 letters

☐ r ☐☐   ☐ r ☐☐   ☐☐ r ☐

☐☐ r ☐   ☐ r ☐☐   ☐☐ r ☐

☐☐☐ r   r ☐☐☐   ☐☐☐ r

Puzzle 151

MEDIUM

7 letters

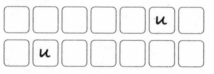

5 letters

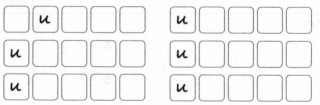

4 letters

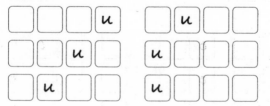

Puzzle 152

7 letters

⬜⬜⬜⬜ c ⬜⬜

6 letters

⬜⬜⬜ c ⬜   ⬜⬜ c ⬜⬜

5 letters

c ⬜⬜⬜⬜   ⬜⬜ c ⬜

c ⬜⬜⬜⬜   ⬜⬜ c ⬜

⬜⬜ c ⬜⬜

4 letters

⬜ c ⬜⬜   c ⬜⬜⬜   ⬜ c ⬜

⬜ c ⬜⬜   c ⬜⬜⬜   ⬜⬜ c ⬜

c ⬜⬜⬜   ⬜⬜ c ⬜

c ⬜⬜⬜   ⬜⬜ c ⬜

Puzzle 153

7 letters

f _ _ _ _ _ _

6 letters

_ _ f _ _ _

5 letters

_ f _ _ _

4 letters

f _ _ _   f _ _ _

f _ _ _   f _ _ _

f _ _ _   f _ _ _

f _ _ _   _ _ f _

f _ _ _   _ _ _ f

f _ _ _   _ _ _ f

Puzzle 154

7 letters

h

6 letters

h

5 letters

h | h

h | h

h | h

4 letters

h | h | h

h | h | h

h | h | h

h | h | h

Puzzle 155

MEDIUM

7 letters

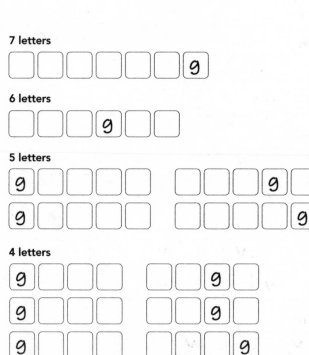

6 letters

5 letters

4 letters

Puzzle 156

7 letters

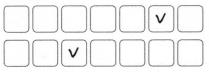

6 letters

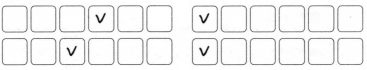

5 letters

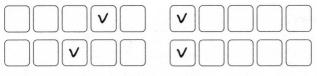

4 letters

Puzzle 157

7 letters

⬜⬜⬜⬜⬜*g*⬜

6 letters

⬜⬜*g*⬜⬜⬜   *g*⬜⬜⬜⬜⬜

⬜⬜*g*⬜⬜⬜

5 letters

⬜⬜⬜*g*⬜

4 letters

⬜*g*⬜⬜   *g*⬜⬜⬜

⬜⬜⬜*g*   *g*⬜⬜⬜

g⬜⬜⬜   ⬜⬜*g*⬜

Puzzle 158

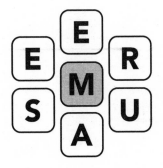

7 letters

m _ _ _ _ _ _

6 letters

_ _ _ _ m _   _ _ _ m _ _

5 letters

_ m _ _ _   _ _ _ m _

m _ _ _ _   _ _ _ _ m

m _ _ _ _   _ m _ _ _

4 letters

_ _ m _   m _ _ _   _ _ _ m

_ m _ _   _ _ m _   _ _ _ m

m _ _ _   _ _ _ m

m _ _ _   _ _ m _

161

Puzzle 159

MEDIUM

7 letters

6 letters

5 letters

4 letters

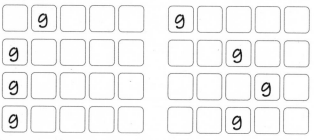

Puzzle 160

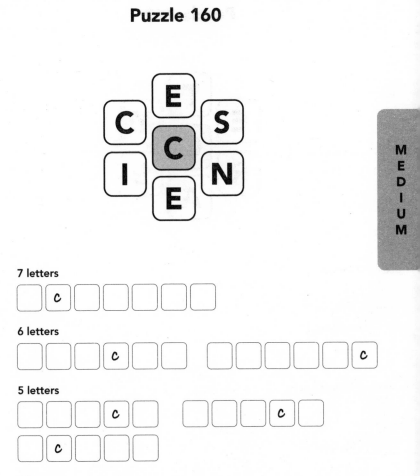

7 letters

☐ c ☐ ☐ ☐ ☐ ☐

6 letters

☐ ☐ ☐ c ☐ ☐   ☐ ☐ ☐ ☐ ☐ c

5 letters

☐ ☐ ☐ c ☐   ☐ ☐ ☐ c ☐

☐ c ☐ ☐ ☐

4 letters

☐ c ☐ ☐   ☐ ☐ c ☐

Puzzle 161

7 letters

⬜ f ⬜ ⬜ ⬜ ⬜ ⬜

6 letters

⬜ ⬜ f ⬜ ⬜ ⬜   ⬜ f ⬜ ⬜ ⬜ ⬜

5 letters

f ⬜ ⬜ ⬜ ⬜   ⬜ f ⬜ ⬜ ⬜

4 letters

⬜ ⬜ ⬜ f   f ⬜ ⬜ ⬜

f ⬜ ⬜ ⬜   ⬜ ⬜ f ⬜

f ⬜ ⬜ ⬜   ⬜ ⬜ f ⬜

f ⬜ ⬜ ⬜

Puzzle 162

7 letters

r _ _ _ _ _ _

6 letters

r _ _ _ _ _   _ _ _ _ _ r

r _ _ _ _ _

5 letters

_ _ r _ _   _ _ _ r _

_ r _ _ _   r _ _ _ _

_ _ _ _ r

4 letters

_ _ r _   _ _ _ r   r _ _ _

_ _ r _   r _ _ _   _ _ _ r

_ r _ _   r _ _ _   _ _ _ r

Puzzle 163

7 letters

6 letters

5 letters

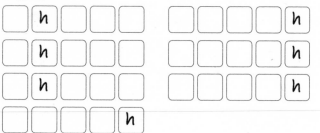

4 letters

Puzzle 164

7 letters

◻◻◻ m ◻◻◻

6 letters

◻ m ◻◻◻◻   ◻◻ m ◻◻◻

5 letters

◻ m ◻◻◻   m ◻◻◻◻

◻◻ m ◻◻   ◻◻◻ m ◻

◻◻ m ◻◻   ◻ m ◻◻◻

4 letters

◻◻ m ◻   ◻◻ m ◻

◻◻ m ◻   m ◻◻◻

◻ m ◻◻   ◻◻◻ m

◻◻ m ◻

Puzzle 165

E
X
P
E
R
T

7 letters

6 letters

5 letters

4 letters

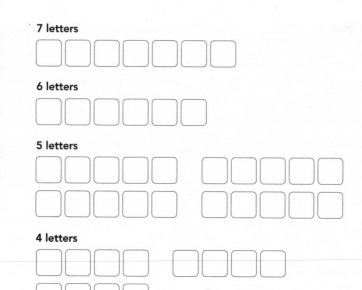

Puzzle 166

7 letters

6 letters

5 letters

4 letters

E X P E R T

Puzzle 167

7 letters

5 letters

4 letters

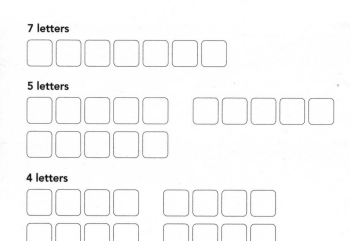

170

Puzzle 168

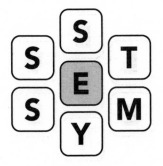

7 letters

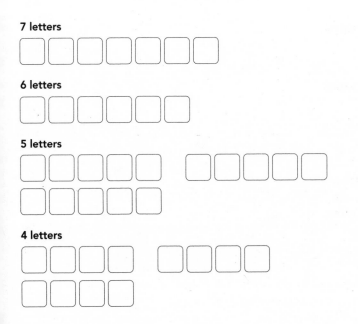

6 letters

5 letters

4 letters

Puzzle 169

7 letters

5 letters

4 letters

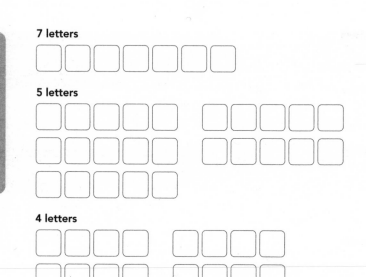

Puzzle 170

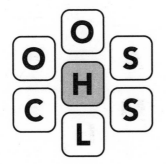

7 letters

6 letters

5 letters

4 letters

Puzzle 171

7 letters

6 letters

5 letters

4 letters

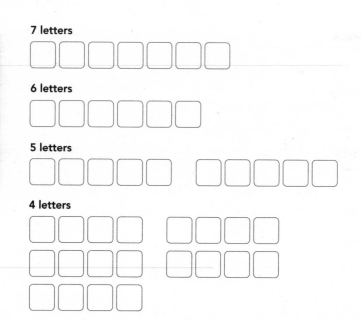

Puzzle 172

7 letters

6 letters

5 letters

4 letters

Puzzle 173

7 letters

6 letters

5 letters

4 letters

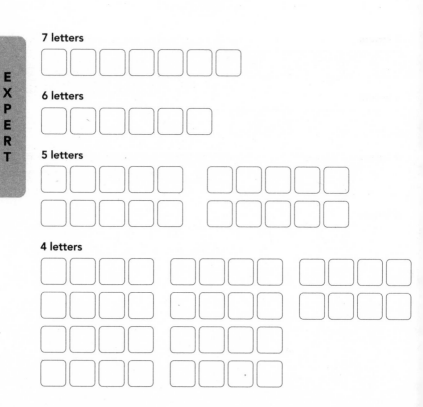

Puzzle 174

7 letters

6 letters

5 letters

4 letters

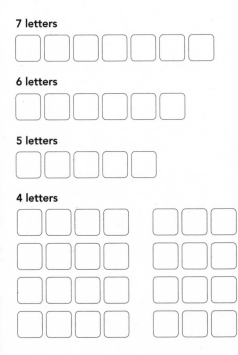

Puzzle 175

7 letters

6 letters

5 letters

4 letters

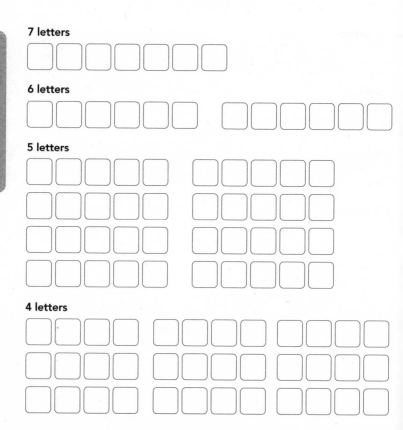

Puzzle 176

7 letters

6 letters

5 letters

4 letters

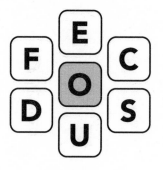

7 letters

6 letters

5 letters

4 letters

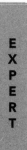

EXPERT

Puzzle 178

7 letters

6 letters

5 letters

4 letters

Puzzle 179

7 letters

6 letters

5 letters

4 letters

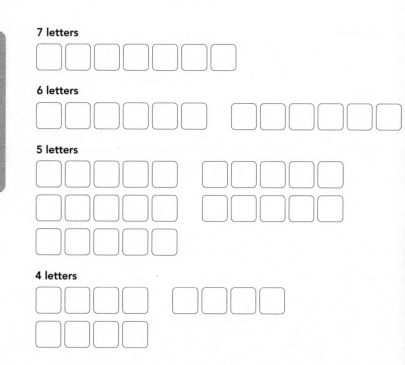

7 letters

6 letters

5 letters

4 letters

Puzzle 181

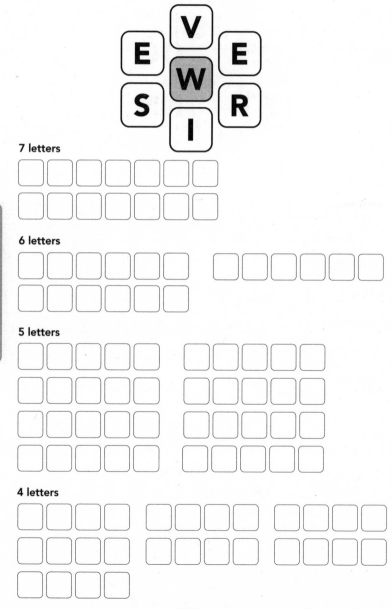

7 letters

6 letters

5 letters

4 letters

Puzzle 182

7 letters

5 letters

4 letters

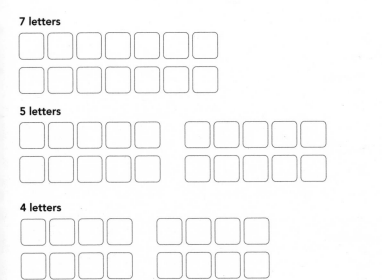

Puzzle 183

7 letters

5 letters

4 letters

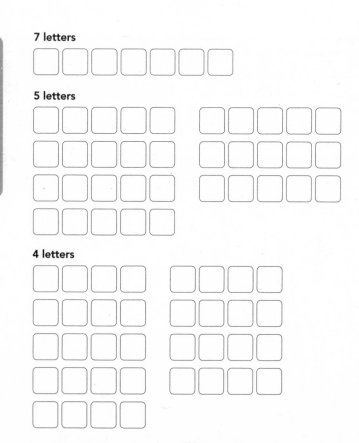

Puzzle 184

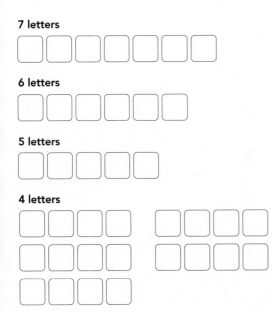

7 letters

6 letters

5 letters

4 letters

Puzzle 185

7 letters

6 letters

5 letters

4 letters

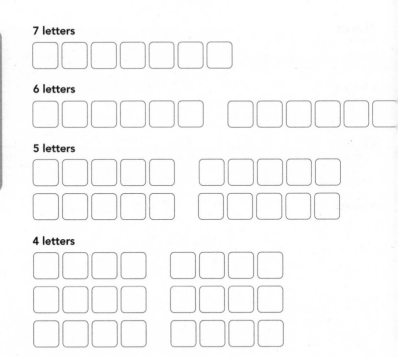

Puzzle 186

7 letters

6 letters

5 letters

4 letters

Puzzle 187

EXPERT

7 letters

6 letters

5 letters

4 letters

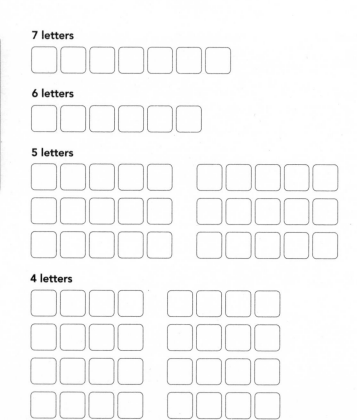

190

7 letters

6 letters

5 letters

4 letters

Puzzle 189

7 letters

6 letters

5 letters

4 letters

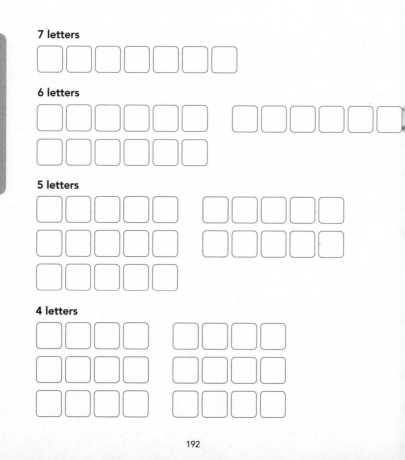

Puzzle 190

7 letters

6 letters

5 letters

4 letters

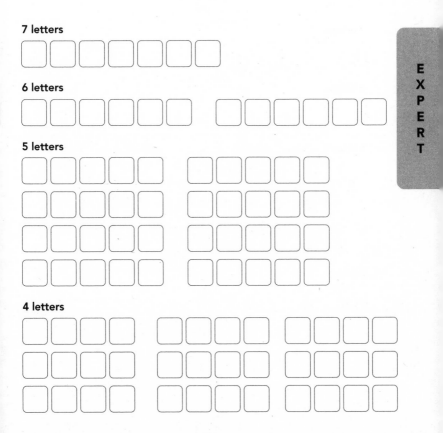

Puzzle 191

7 letters

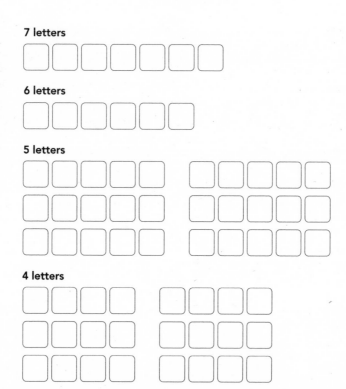

6 letters

5 letters

4 letters

Puzzle 192

7 letters

5 letters

4 letters

Puzzle 193

7 letters

6 letters

5 letters

4 letters

Puzzle 194

7 letters

5 letters

4 letters

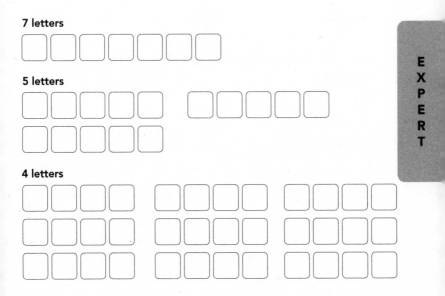

Puzzle 195

7 letters

5 letters

4 letters

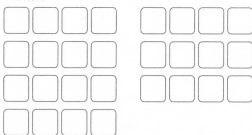

Puzzle 196

7 letters

5 letters

4 letters

Puzzle 197

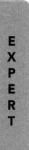

7 letters

6 letters

5 letters

4 letters

Puzzle 198

7 letters

6 letters

5 letters

4 letters

Puzzle 199

7 letters

6 letters

5 letters

4 letters

Puzzle 200

7 letters

6 letters

5 letters

4 letters

Puzzle 201

7 letters

5 letters

4 letters

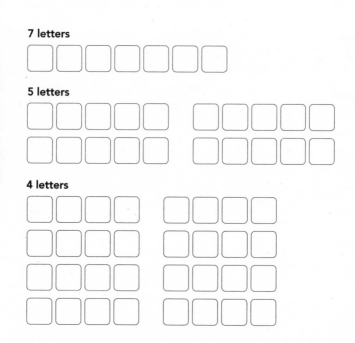

Puzzle 202

7 letters

6 letters

5 letters

4 letters

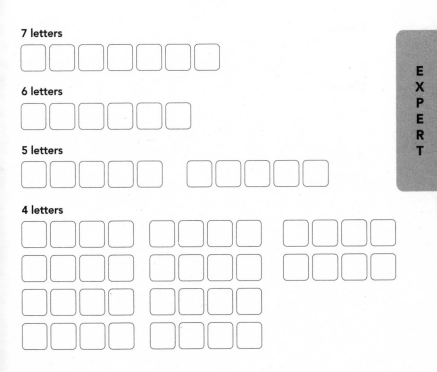

Puzzle 203

7 letters

5 letters

4 letters

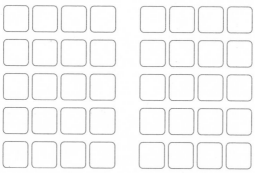

Puzzle 204

7 letters

6 letters

5 letters

4 letters

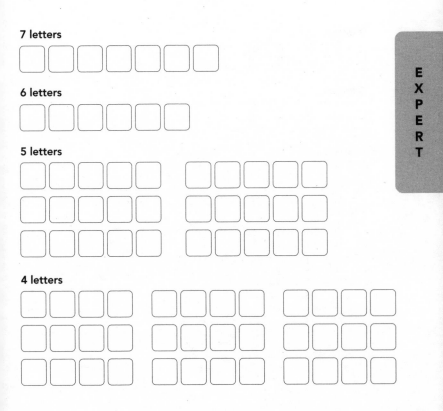

E
X
P
E
R
T

Puzzle 205

7 letters

6 letters

5 letters

4 letters

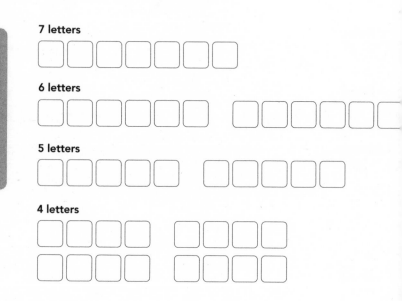

Puzzle 206

7 letters

6 letters

5 letters

4 letters

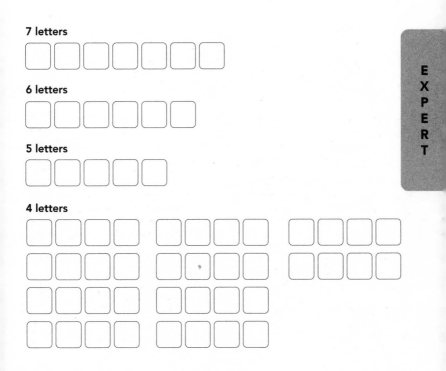

Puzzle 207

EXPERT

7 letters

6 letters

5 letters

4 letters

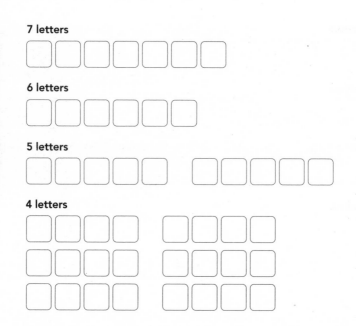

Puzzle 208

7 letters

6 letters

5 letters

4 letters

Puzzle 209

7 letters

6 letters

5 letters

4 letters

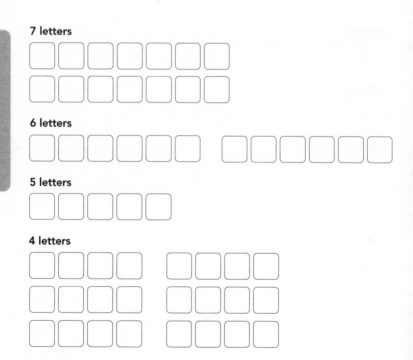

Puzzle 210

7 letters

6 letters

5 letters

4 letters

Puzzle 211

7 letters

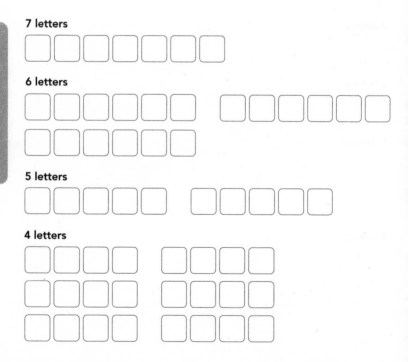

6 letters

5 letters

4 letters

Puzzle 212

7 letters

6 letters

5 letters

4 letters

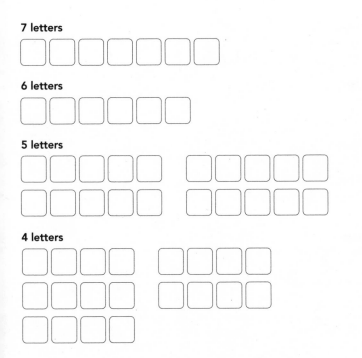

Puzzle 213

7 letters

6 letters

5 letters

4 letters

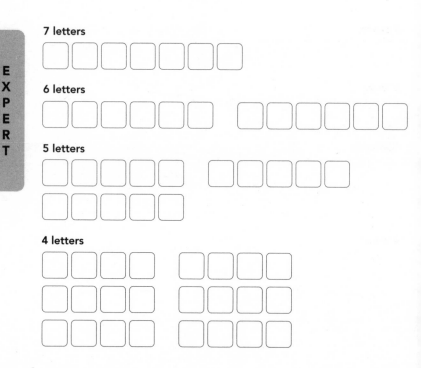

Puzzle 214

7 letters

6 letters

5 letters

4 letters

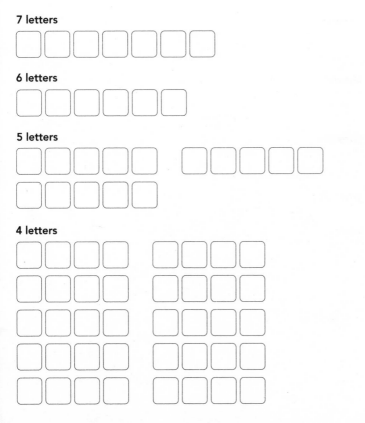

Puzzle 215

7 letters

6 letters

5 letters

4 letters

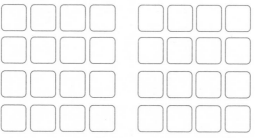

Puzzle 216

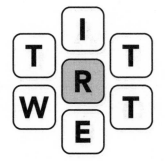

7 letters

6 letters

5 letters

4 letters

Puzzle 217

7 letters

5 letters

4 letters

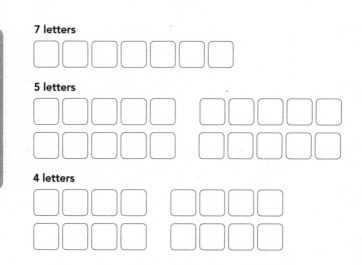

7 letters

6 letters

5 letters

4 letters

Puzzle 219

7 letters

6 letters

5 letters

4 letters

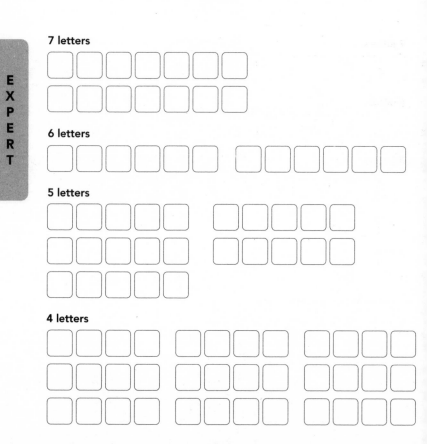

Puzzle 220

7 letters

5 letters

4 letters

Puzzle 221

7 letters

6 letters

5 letters

4 letters

Puzzle 222

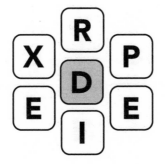

7 letters

5 letters

4 letters

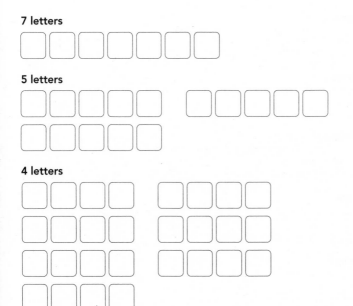

Puzzle 223

7 letters

6 letters

5 letters

4 letters

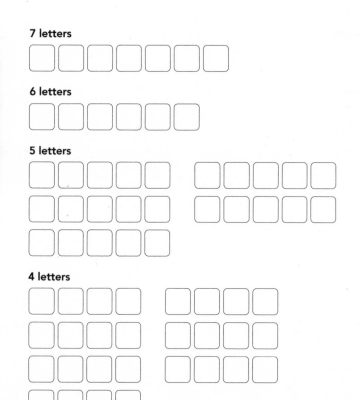

Puzzle 224

7 letters

6 letters

5 letters

4 letters

Puzzle 225

E
X
P
E
R
T

7 letters

6 letters

5 letters

4 letters

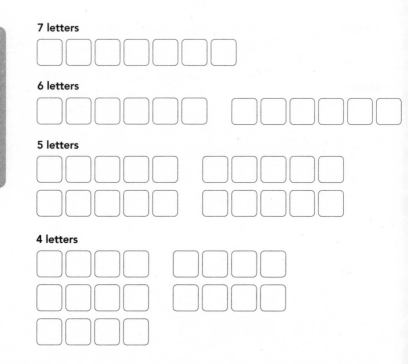

Puzzle 226

7 letters

6 letters

5 letters

4 letters

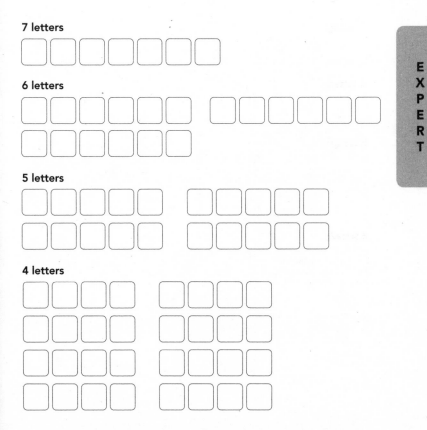

Puzzle 227

7 letters

6 letters

5 letters

4 letters

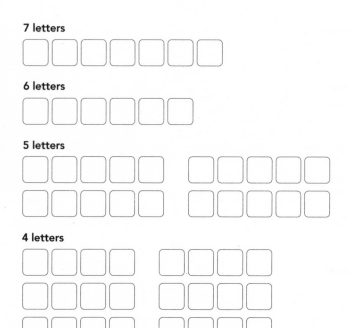

Puzzle 228

7 letters

6 letters

5 letters

4 letters

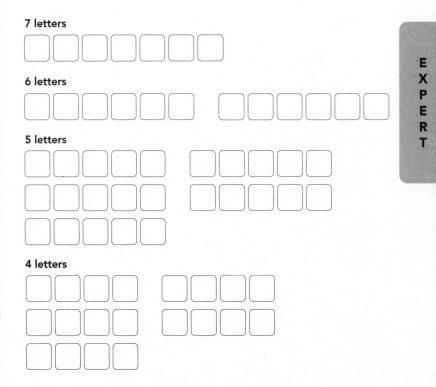

Puzzle 229

7 letters

6 letters

5 letters

4 letters

Puzzle 230

7 letters

6 letters

5 letters

4 letters

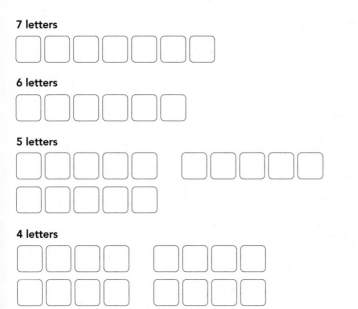

Puzzle 231

7 letters

6 letters

5 letters

4 letters

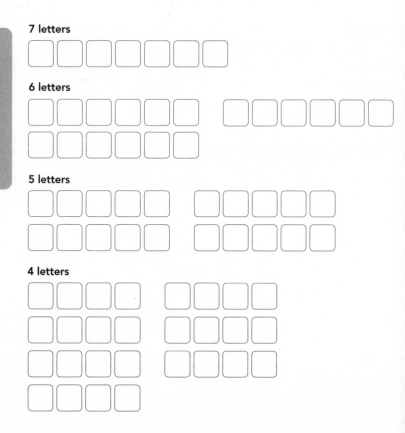

234

Puzzle 232

7 letters

5 letters

4 letters

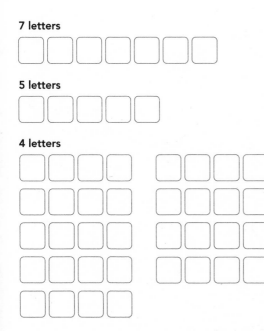

Puzzle 233

7 letters

6 letters

5 letters

4 letters

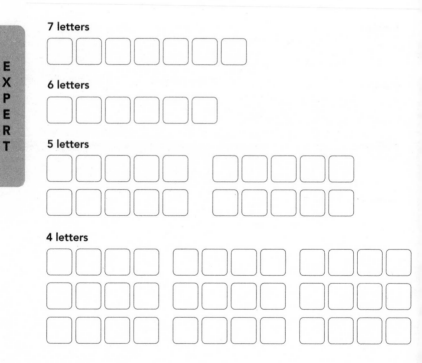

Puzzle 234

7 letters

6 letters

5 letters

4 letters

Puzzle 235

7 letters

6 letters

5 letters

4 letters

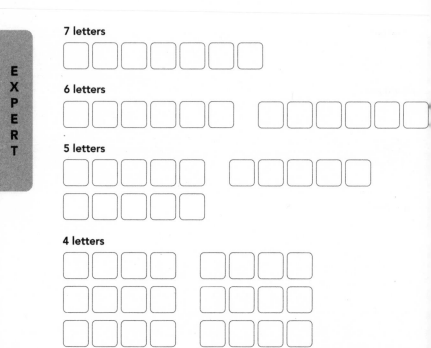

Puzzle 236

7 letters

6 letters

5 letters

4 letters

Puzzle 237

7 letters

5 letters

4 letters

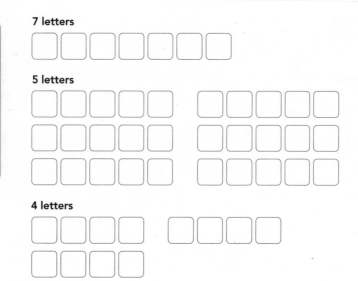

Puzzle 238

7 letters

6 letters

5 letters

4 letters

Puzzle 239

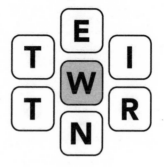

7 letters

6 letters

5 letters

4 letters

Puzzle 240

7 letters

6 letters

5 letters

4 letters

Puzzle 241

7 letters

6 letters

5 letters

4 letters

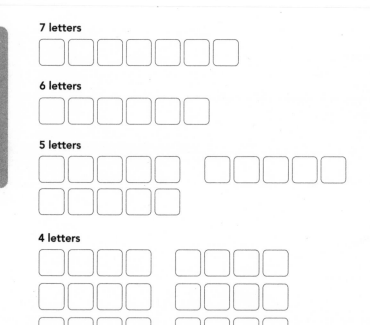

Puzzle 242

7 letters

6 letters

5 letters

4 letters

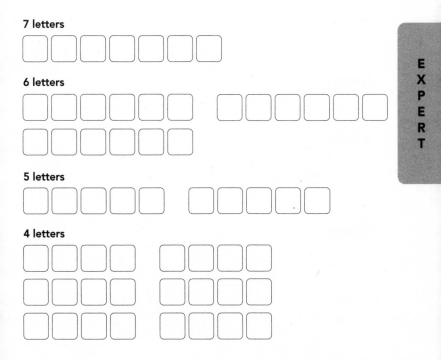

Puzzle 243

7 letters

6 letters

5 letters

4 letters

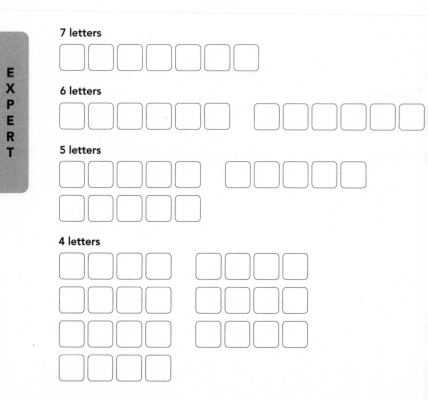

Puzzle 244

7 letters

6 letters

5 letters

4 letters

Solutions

Puzzle 1
7 – excited
6 – deceit, excite
5 – cited, edict
4 – cede, cite, dice, iced

Puzzle 2
7 – assault
5 – atlas, lasts, lusts, salsa, salts, slats
4 – alas, lass, last, lust, salt, slat

Puzzle 3
7 – evening
6 – engine
5 – genie, given
4 – even, gene, nine, vein, vine

Puzzle 4
7 – balance
5 – banal, cabal, cable
4 – able, bale, bane, bean

Puzzle 5
7 – causing
5 – cuing, suing, using
4 – anus, gnus, guns, snug, sung

Puzzle 6
7 – parking
6 – raking
5 – prank
4 – akin, king, knap, park, pink, rank, rink

Puzzle 7
7 – enables
6 – enable
5 – bales, beans, blase
4 – able, bale, bane, bans, base, bean, been, bees, nabs, slab

Puzzle 8
7 – kidneys
6 – kidney
5 – dinky, dykes, inked, kinds, skein, skied
4 – desk, disk, dyke, inks, inky, keys, kids, kind, sink, skid, skin

Puzzle 9
7 – because
5 – abuse, beaus, cubes, scuba
4 – base, beau, bees, cabs, cube, cubs, scab

Puzzle 10
7 – session
6 – noises, nosies
5 – noise, noses
4 – eons, ions, ness, nose, ones, sine, sins, sons

Puzzle 11
7 – removal
6 – marvel, morale
5 – molar, moral, mover, realm
4 – lame, loam, male, mare, marl, meal, mole, more, move, ream, roam

Puzzle 12
7 – covered
6 – recode
5 – coder, cored, coved, cover, creed
4 – cede, code, coed, cord, core, cove

Puzzle 13
7 – seeking
5 – eking, kings, knees, skein
4 – ekes, geek, inks, keen, kegs, king, knee, seek, sink, skin

Puzzle 14
7 – removed
6 – remove
5 – moved, mover
4 – deem, dome, mere, mode, more, move

Puzzle 15
7 – clarity
6 – racily
5 – lyric
4 – airy, arty, city, clay, lacy, racy, tray

Puzzle 16
7 – employs
6 – employ, myopes
5 – moles, mopes, myope, poems
4 – elms, mole, mope, mops, poem, some

Puzzle 17
7 – develop
6 – eloped
5 – elope, loped, poled
4 – deep, dope, lope, peel, pled, plod, pole

Puzzle 18
7 – derived
6 – deride, derive
5 – dived, diver, dried, drive, eider
4 – deed, deer, died, dire, dive, ever, reed, ride, veer, vied

Puzzle 19
7 – edition
6 – iodine
5 – idiot, noted, toned
4 – done, dote, node, note, toed, tone

Puzzle 20
7 – brought
6 – bought, trough
5 – bough, grout, ought, rough, tough
4 – bout, gout, grub, hour, hurt, rout, thug, tour

Puzzle 21
7 – depends
6 – depend
5 – deeps, speed, spend
4 – deep, pens, seep, sped

Puzzle 22
7 – contest
6 – octets
5 – cents, cones, octet, scent, scone
4 – cent, cone, cons, cost, cots, once, scot, sect

Puzzle 23
7 – founded
6 – fondue, funded
5 – found, unfed
4 – done, dune, fend, feud, fond, fund, node, nude, undo

Puzzle 24
7 – flowers, fowlers
6 – flower, fowler, lowers, slower
5 – lores, loser, lower, resow, roles, sower, swore, worse
4 – fore, lore, ores, role, rose, rows, serf, sore, wore

Puzzle 25
7 – holding
6 – doling
5 – dingo, doing
4 – ding, dong, gild, gold, hind, hold, idol, lido

Puzzle 26
7 – growing
6 – goring, rowing
5 – going, groin, grown, owing, wring, wrong
4 – gong, gown, grin, grog, grow, ring, wing

Puzzle 27
7 – athlete
5 – lathe, teeth
4 – hale, halt, hate, heal, heat, heel, that

Puzzle 28
7 – classes
6 – lasses, scales
5 – class, laces, sales, scale, seals
4 – ales, lace, lass, leas, less, sale, seal

Puzzle 29
7 – treated
6 – teared
5 – dater, deter, rated, trade, tread
4 – dare, dart, date, dear, deer, drat, read, reed

Puzzle 30
7 – convert
6 – cornet, covert, vector
5 – coven, cover, covet, crone, recto
4 – cent, cone, core, corn, cove, once

Puzzle 31
7 – planned
6 – panned, planed
5 – paled, panel, pedal, penal, plane, plead
4 – leap, nape, pale, pane, peal, plan, plea, pled

Puzzle 32
7 – monitor
6 – motion
4 – into, mint, omit, onto, riot, root, torn, trim, trio

Puzzle 33
7 – musical
6 – claims
5 – claim, mails, music
4 – aims, calm, mail, slim

Puzzle 34
7 – needles
6 – lensed, needle
5 – denes, dense, lends, needs
4 – dens, eels, else, ends, lees, lens, seed, seen, send, sled

Puzzle 35
7 – include
6 – induce
5 – dunce, indue, lined, lucid
4 – cued, dice, dine, duel, dune, iced, idle, lend, lied, nude

Puzzle 36
7 – insight
6 – nights, siting, things
5 – night, sight, sting, thing, tings
4 – gins, gist, nigh, sigh, sign, sing, ting

Puzzle 37
7 – seasons
6 – season
5 – aeons, noses, oases
4 – aeon, eons, nose, ones, sons

Puzzle 38
7 – combine
6 – income
5 – mince
4 – coin, comb, come, cone, icon, mice, nice, once

Puzzle 39
7 – absence
6 – encase, seance
5 – beans, canes, cease, scene
4 – aces, acne, bane, base, bean, been, bees, cane, case, ease, sane, seen

Puzzle 40
7 – adopted
5 – adept, adopt, dated, depot, doted, opted, taped
4 – atop, date, dote, pate, peat, poet, tape, toad, toed

Puzzle 41
7 – browser
6 – bowers, browse, rowers
5 – bower, brews, brows, resow, rower, sower, swore, worse
4 – bows, brew, brow, ower, owes, rows, webs, woes, wore

Puzzle 42
7 – average
6 – greave, ravage
5 – agave, grave, reuse, verge
4 – aver, ever, gave, rave, veer

Puzzle 43
7 – esquire, queries
6 – risque, squire
5 – reuse
4 – rise, rues, ruse, seer, sire, suer, sure, user

Puzzle 44
7 – perfect, prefect
5 – creep, crepe, crept, erect, peter
4 – free, fret, peer, pert, reef, tree

Puzzle 45
7 – unified
5 – fiend, fined, indie, indue, unfed
4 – dine, dune, fend, feud, fine, nude

Puzzle 46
7 – veteran
6 – tavern
5 – avert, event, nerve, never, raven
4 – aver, eave, even, ever, nave, rave, vane, veer, vent

Puzzle 47
7 – biggest
5 – bites
4 – begs, best, bets, bite, bits

Puzzle 48
7 – outputs
6 – output
5 – pouts, putts, spout
4 – opts, opus, post, pots, pout, puts, putt, soup, spot, stop, tops

Puzzle 49
7 – serious
6 – issuer, rouses
5 – issue, roses, rouse, sours, souse, users
4 – ours, ruse, sour, suer, sues, sure, user, uses

Puzzle 50
7 – uniform
6 – inform, unfirm
5 – forum, minor, mourn
4 – firm, form, four, from, morn, norm

Puzzle 51
7 – surgery
6 – urgers
5 – greys, surge, urger, urges
4 – grey, guys, rugs, urge

Puzzle 52
7 – prevent
6 – repent
5 – enter, event, nerve, never, preen, terne
4 – even, ever, pent, rent, teen, tern, tree, veer, vent

Puzzle 53
7 – telling
6 – tingle
5 – gilet, glint, ingle, tinge
4 – gill, gilt, glen, ting

Puzzle 54
7 – reflect
6 – refect
5 – cleft, fleet
4 – clef, feel, feet, felt, fete, flee, free, fret, left, reef

Puzzle 55
7 – consult
6 – consul, counts
5 – count, snout
4 – cons, nous, nuts, onus, snot, stun, tons, tuns, unto

Puzzle 56
7 – analyst
6 – aslant
5 – antsy, nasal, nasty, natal, satan, slant
4 – anal, ants, tans

Puzzle 57
7 – applied
6 – lipped
5 – ailed, ideal, piled, piped, plaid, plied
4 – aide, dial, idea, idle, laid, lied, paid, pail, pied, pile, pipe

Puzzle 58
7 – opening
6 – pigeon
5 – opine
4 – gone, neon, nine, none, open, pine

Puzzle 59
7 – offices
6 – office
5 – coifs, fifes, scoff
4 – coif, fife, foci, foes

Puzzle 60
7 – mention
4 – emit, item, mien, mine, mint, mite, mote, omen, omit, time, tome

Puzzle 61
7 – numbers
6 – number
5 – berms, burns, numbs, umber
4 – berm, bums, buns, burn, nubs, numb, rubs, snub

Puzzle 62
7 – origins
6 – groins, origin
5 – groin, irons
4 – ions, iron, noir, snog, song

Puzzle 63
7 – charges
6 – charge, graces
5 – cages, crags, gears, grace, rages
4 – ages, cage, crag, gash, gear, hags, rage, rags, sage, shag

Puzzle 64
7 – produce
6 – recoup
5 – coder, coped, coper, cored, coupe, croup, crude, cured, decor
4 – code, coed, cope, cord, core, coup, crop, cued, curd, cure, ecru

S
O
L
U
T
I
O
N
S

Puzzle 65
7 – careful
6 – earful, fulcra
5 – facer, farce, feral, flare
4 – cafe, calf, clef, face, fare, fear, flea, flue, fuel, furl, leaf

Puzzle 66
7 – interim
6 – minter, remint
5 – merit, miner, mitre, remit, timer
4 – emit, item, mine, mint, mire, mite, term, time, trim

Puzzle 67
7 – walking
6 – waking, waling
5 – align, awing
4 – akin, gain, kiln, king, lain, link, nail, wail, wing, wink

Puzzle 68
7 – coaches
6 – caches
5 – aches, cache, chaos, chase, chose, coach
4 – aces, ache, case, cash, each, echo

Puzzle 69
7 – playing
6 – paling, paying, plying
5 – aping, plain
4 – pail, pain, pang, ping, plan, play

Puzzle 70
7 – farmers, framers
6 – farmer, framer, frames
5 – fares, farms, fears, frame, safer
4 – fame, fare, farm, fear, safe, serf

Puzzle 71
7 – working
6 – rowing
5 – grown, owing, wring, wrong
4 – gown, grow, know, wing, wink, work, worn

Puzzle 72
7 – profile
6 – pilfer
5 – peril
4 – flip, flop, lope, pier, pile, pole, pore, ripe, rope

Puzzle 73
7 – goddess
6 – dodges
5 – doges, dosed, doses
4 – does, dogs, dose, egos, gods, goes, odds, odes, sods

Puzzle 74
7 – upwards
6 – upward
5 – draws, wards, warps, wraps
4 – draw, paws, swap, wads, ward, warp, wars, wasp, wrap

Puzzle 75
7 – episode
6 – espied, poised
5 – poise, spied
4 – dies, dips, ides, pied, pies, side

Puzzle 76
7 – glowing
6 – lowing, ogling
5 – going, lingo, login, owing
4 – glow, gong, gown, long, wing

Puzzle 77
7 – capable
6 – palace
5 – apace, cabal, cable, place
4 – cape, clap, lace, pace

Puzzle 78
7 – factory
6 – crafty
5 – foray, forty, oracy
4 – arty, fray, racy, tray

Puzzle 79
7 – updated
6 – update
5 – adept, dated, duped, taped
4 – aped, date, dead, duet, dupe

Puzzle 80
7 – reworks, workers
6 – rework, worker
5 – resow, rower, sower, swore, works, worse
4 – owes, rows, skew, woes, woke, wore, work

Puzzle 81
7 – arrived
6 – arrive, driver, varied
5 – diver, drive, raved, raver, river
4 – avid, diva, dive, rave, rive, vied

Puzzle 82
7 – payment
5 – empty, peaty
4 – nape, pane, pant, pate, peat, pent, tamp, tape, type

Puzzle 83
7 – illness
5 – lines
4 – lens, line, ness, sine, sins

Puzzle 84
7 – typical
5 – plait, typic
4 – city, clip, pity, tail

Puzzle 85
7 – emotion
6 – motion
4 – moon, moot, mote, omen, omit, tome

Puzzle 86
7 – example
5 – ample, maple
4 – exam, lame, lamp, male, meal, palm

Puzzle 87
7 – receive
5 – eerie, reeve
4 – ever, rice, rive, veer, vice

Puzzle 88
7 – logging
6 – ogling
5 – going, lingo
4 – gong, lion, loin, long

Puzzle 89
7 – visible
5 – evils, lives, veils
4 – evil, live, veil, vies, vile

Puzzle 90
7 – cooking
6 – coking, cooing
4 – coin, cook, icon, nock, nook

Puzzle 91
7 – arrange
6 – garner, ranger
5 – anger, range
4 – gear, rage, rang

Puzzle 92
7 – finally
5 – filly, final, flail
4 – fail, fall, fill, flan, flay

Puzzle 93
7 – economy
5 – money, moony
4 – come, cone, moon, omen, once

Puzzle 94
7 – confirm
6 – inform, micron
5 – minor
4 – firm, form, from, morn, norm

Puzzle 95
7 – follows
6 – follow
5 – flows, fowls, woofs
4 – flow, fowl, wolf, woof

Puzzle 96
7 – falling
5 – final, fling
4 – fail, fall, fang, fill, flag, flan

Puzzle 97
7 – company
6 – canopy
4 – coma, copy, moan, pony

Puzzle 98
7 – verdict
6 – divert
5 – diver, drive, evict, rivet
4 – dive, rive, vice, vied

Puzzle 99
7 – obliged
6 – bilged, boiled, oblige
5 – bilge, bogie, geoid, gibed, glide, oiled
4 – bide, bile, boil, gibe, gild, glib, idle, idol, lido, lied

Puzzle 100
7 – jealous
6 – joules
5 – joule, louse
4 – aloe, also, lose, sloe, sole, soul

Puzzle 101
7 – builder, rebuild
6 – buried
5 – blued, bluer, build, lured, lurid, ruled
4 – blue, blur, burl, duel, lieu, lure, rude, rule

Puzzle 102
7 – fishing
6 – finish
5 – finis
4 – figs, fins, fish, gins, nigh, shin, sigh, sign, sing

Puzzle 103
7 – beaches
5 – aches, beach, beech, cease, chase
4 – aces, ache, cabs, case, cash, each, scab

Puzzle 104
7 – forever
5 – fever, freer, refer, rover
4 – ever, fore, free, over, reef, rove, veer

Puzzle 105
7 – history
6 – shirty
5 – horsy, story
4 – hoys, rosy, toys

Puzzle 106
7 – closely
6 – cellos, solely
5 – cello, close
4 – cloy, cole, cosy, lose, sloe, sole

Puzzle 107
7 – guessed
6 – sedges, suedes
5 – edges, guess, sedge, seeds, suede
4 – dues, edge, geed, gees, seed, sees, sued, sues, used, uses

Puzzle 108
7 – contain
6 – action, atonic, cannot, canton, incant, tannic
5 – antic, canon, canto, tonic
4 – cant, coat, coin, icon, taco

Puzzle 109
7 – holiday
5 – daily, doily
4 – ahoy, holy, idly, idyl, lady, oily

Puzzle 110
7 – capital
6 – capita
5 – plait
4 – clap, clip, pact, pail, plat

Puzzle 111
7 – meaning
6 – enigma, naming
5 – gamin, image, mange
4 – amen, game, magi, main, mane, mean, mine, name

Puzzle 112
7 – beliefs
6 – belief
5 – feels, files, flees, flies
4 – beef, feel, fees, fibs, file, flee, life, self

Puzzle 113
7 – delimit, limited
5 – demit, limit, tilde, tiled, timed, timid
4 – diet, edit, emit, item, mite, tide, tied, tile, time

Puzzle 114
7 – muscles
6 – muscle, mussel
5 – mules, muses, scums, slums
4 – elms, emus, mess, mule, muse, muss, scum, slum, sums

Puzzle 115
7 – circles, clerics
6 – circle, cleric, relics, slicer
5 – cries, relic, slice
4 – ices, lice, rice

Puzzle 116
7 – control
5 – colon, croon
4 – clot, colt, cool, coot, corn, loon, loot, onto, root, tool, toon, torn

Puzzle 117
7 – greeted
6 – degree
5 – deter, edger, greed
4 – deer, dreg, edge, geed, reed

Puzzle 118
7 – feeling, fleeing
6 – feline
5 – elfin, feign, fling, genie, liege
4 – file, fine, life, line

Puzzle 119
7 – infants
6 – faints, infant
5 – faint
4 – fans, fast, fats, fins, fist, fits, sift

Puzzle 120
7 – deducer, reduced
6 – deduce, reduce
5 – ceded, creed, crude, cured, deuce
4 – cede, cued, curd, cure

Puzzle 121
7 – outfits
6 – outfit, outsit
5 – stout, touts, tufts
4 – oust, suit, tout, tuft

Puzzle 122
7 – tickets
6 – ticket
5 – kites, stick, ticks
4 – kite, kits, sick, skit, tick, tike

Puzzle 123
7 – drivers
6 – divers, driver, drives, rivers
5 – diver, dives, drive, river
4 – dive, revs, vied, vies

Puzzle 124
7 – drawing, warding
6 – inward, wading
5 – awing, drawn, wring
4 – dawn, draw, gnaw, wand, ward, warn, wind, wing

Puzzle 125
7 – ancient
6 – canine
5 – antic, enact
4 – acne, cane, cant, cent, cite, nice

Puzzle 126
7 – meeting, teeming
6 – meting
4 – emit, item, meet, mete, mine, mint, mite, teem, time

Puzzle 127
7 – imagery
6 – gamier, mirage
5 – gamer, gayer, grime, grimy, image
4 – game, gamy, gear, germ, gram, grey, grim, magi, rage

Puzzle 128
7 – notably
6 – botany
5 – baton, bloat, nobly
4 – ably, blot, boat, bolt, bony

Puzzle 129
7 – beloved
5 – bleed, delve, lobed, loved
4 – bled, bode, bold, dole, dove, lode

Puzzle 130
7 – goodies
6 – geoids
5 – geoid, goods, goose
4 – digs, dogs, egos, gods, goes, good

Puzzle 131
7 – stadium
6 – admits, amidst, audits, autism
5 – admit, audit, maids, midst, staid
4 – aids, aims, amid, dais, dims, maid, mist, said, suit

Puzzle 132
7 – weather, wreathe
6 – wether, wreath
5 – threw, water, wheat, where, wrath
4 – thaw, twee, ware, wart, wear, were, what, whet

Puzzle 133
7 – species
6 – espies, pieces, specie, spices
5 – epics, piece, seeps, specs, spice, spies
4 – epic, pies, seep, sips, spec

Puzzle 134
7 – servers
6 – server, serves, severs, verses
5 – serve, sever, veers, verse
4 – ever, revs, veer

Puzzle 135
7 – variety
6 – verity
5 – avert, rivet
4 – rave, vary, very

Puzzle 136
7 – country
6 – county, outcry
5 – corny, crony
4 – your, yurt

Puzzle 137
7 – chamber
6 – breach, camber
5 – amber, beach, brace, bream
4 – bare, beam, bear, berm, brae, crab, herb

Puzzle 138
7 – station
5 – iotas, stoat, toast
4 – ions, iota, oast, oats, snot, tons, tots

Puzzle 139
7 – promote
6 – trompe
5 – motor, tempo
4 – moor, moot, mope, more, mote, perm, poem, romp, room, term, tome

Puzzle 140
7 – careers
6 – career, crease, racers
5 – acres, carer, cares, racer, races, scare, scree
4 – aces, acre, arcs, care, cars, case, race, scar

Puzzle 141
7 – connect
5 – nonet
4 – cone, cent, neon, none, note, once, tone

Puzzle 142
7 – perform
6 – former, reform, romper
5 – roper
4 – fore, form, from, more, perm, pore, romp, rope

Puzzle 143
7 – package
5 – agape, apace
4 – cage, cake, cape, gape, pace, pack, page, peak

Puzzle 144
7 – changes
6 – change, encash
5 – aches, cages, canes, chase
4 – aces, ache, acne, cage, cane, cans, case, cash, each, scan

Puzzle 145
7 – camping
6 – pacing
5 – aping, panic
4 – camp, pain, pang, ping

Puzzle 146
7 – islands
6 – island
5 – dials, lands, sands
4 – aids, dais, dial, dins, lads, laid, land, lids, said, sand, slid

Puzzle 147
7 – exactly
6 – acetyl
5 – cleat, eclat, exact, exalt, latex
4 – axle, celt, lace, late, tale, teal

Puzzle 148
7 – happens
6 – happen, shapen
5 – ashen, napes, panes
4 – hens, nape, naps, pane, pans, pens, snap, span

Puzzle 149
7 – license, silence
6 – nieces
5 – cense, niece, scene, since, slice
4 – ices, lice, nice

Puzzle 150
7 – awarded
6 – warded
5 – adder, award, aware, dared, dread, wader
4 – area, dare, dear, draw, drew, read, ward, ware, wear

Puzzle 151
7 – lineout, outline
5 – tuile, unite, unlit, untie, until, utile
4 – lieu, lout, lute, tune, unit, unto

Puzzle 152
7 – affects
6 – affect, facets
5 – cafes, caste, faces, facet, facts
4 – aces, acts, cafe, case, cast, cats, face, fact, scat, sect

Puzzle 153
7 – feature
6 – refute
5 – after
4 – fare, fate, fear, feat, feet, feta, fete, free, fret, raft, reef, turf

Puzzle 154
7 – hospice
6 – epochs
5 – chips, chops, chose, echos, epoch, hopes
4 – chip, chop, echo, hips, hoes, hope, hops, hose, posh, ship, shoe, shop

Puzzle 155
7 – selling
6 – single
5 – glens, glens, singe, sling
4 – gels, gill, gins, glen, legs, sign, sing

Puzzle 156
7 – deserve, severed
6 – served, severe, veered, versed
5 – serve, sever, veers, verse
4 – ever, revs, veer

Puzzle 157
7 – garbage
6 – bagger, beggar, garage
5 – barge
4 – agar, brag, garb, gear, grab, rage

Puzzle 158
7 – measure
6 – resume, seamer
5 – amuse, mares, meres, reams, serum, smear
4 – arms, emus, mare, mere, muse, rams, ream, same, seam, seem

Puzzle 159
7 – greatly
6 – gyrate
5 – aglet, gayer, glare, grate, great, lager, large, regal
4 – gale, gate, gear, grey, gyre, rage

Puzzle 160
7 – science
6 – nieces, scenic
5 – niece, scene, since
4 – ices, nice

Puzzle 161
7 – officer
6 – coffer, office
5 – force, offer
4 – coif, fife, fire, foci, fore, rife, riff

Puzzle 162
7 – release
6 – resale, reseal, sealer
5 – earls, erase, laser, leers, reels
4 – earl, ears, eras, leer, rase, real, reel, sear, seer

Puzzle 163
7 – cheaper
6 – preach
5 – cheap, cheep, cheer, parch, peach, perch, reach
4 – ache, arch, chap, char, each, hare, heap, hear, here

Puzzle 164
7 – glimpse
6 – impels, simple
5 – impel, limes, limps, miles, slime, smile
4 – elms, gems, imps, lime, limp, mile, slim

Puzzle 165
7 – protect
6 – cotter
5 – crept, coper, octet, recto
4 – cope, core, crop

Puzzle 166
7 – victory
6 – victor
5 – ivory, toric
4 – city, coir, otic, riot, trio

Puzzle 167
7 – believe
5 – belie, bevel, levee
4 – bile, evil, live, veil, vibe, vile

Puzzle 168
7 – systems
6 – system
5 – messy, stems, styes
4 – mess, sets, stem

Puzzle 169
7 – empathy
5 – empty, matey, meaty, peaty, thyme
4 – hype, myth, they, type

Puzzle 170
7 – schools
6 – school
5 – lochs, shoos, slosh
4 – coho, loch, shoo

Puzzle 171
7 – roughly
6 – hourly
5 – ghoul, rough
4 – hour, hurl, ruly, ugly, your

Puzzle 172
7 – attacks
6 – attack
5 – stack, tacks
4 – cask, sack, skat, tack, task

Puzzle 173
7 – concert
6 – cornet
5 – crone, recto, tenor, toner
4 – cent, cone, core, note, once, rent, rote, tern, tone, tore

Puzzle 174
7 – traffic
6 – tariff
5 – craft
4 – fact, fair, fiat, frat, raft, riff, rift, tiff

Puzzle 175
7 – divorce
6 – voiced, voicer
5 – coved, cover, diver, drive, drove, roved, video, voice
4 – cove, dive, dove, over, rive, rove, vice, vied, void

Puzzle 176
7 – talking
6 – taking
5 – kiang
4 – akin, kiln, kilt, king, knit, lank, link, talk, tank

Puzzle 177
7 – defocus, focused
6 – escudo
5 – codes, coeds, douse, focus
4 – code, coed, does, dose, foes, odes

Puzzle 178
7 – service
6 – revise
5 – serve, sever, sieve, veers, verse, vices
4 – ever, revs, veer, vice, vies, vise

Puzzle 179
7 – revenue
6 – evener, veneer
5 – nerve, never, reeve, revue, venue
4 – even, ever, veer

Puzzle 180
7 – wedding
6 – winded, winged
5 – widen, wined
4 – wend, wide, wind, wine, wing

Puzzle 181
7 – reviews, viewers
6 – review, swerve, viewer
5 – ewers, resew, sewer, views, weirs, wires, wiser, wives
4 – ewer, ewes, view, weir, were, wire, wise

Puzzle 182
7 – kitchen, thicken
5 – chink, ketch, thick, think
4 – hick, hike, kite, knit, neck, nick, tick, tike

Puzzle 183
7 – mixture
5 – merit, mitre, mixer, remit, remix, timer, uteri
4 – emit, item, mire, mite, mute, rime, term, time, trim

Puzzle 184
7 – forward
6 – farrow
5 – arrow
4 – ford, road, roar, woad, word

Puzzle 185
7 – viruses
6 – issuer, versus
5 – issue, ruses, users, virus
4 – rues, ruse, sues, sure, user, uses

Puzzle 186
7 – faculty
6 – faulty
5 – fatly, fault
4 – calf, caul, clay, fact, flat, flay, lacy, talc

Puzzle 187
7 – culture
6 – cutler
5 – cruel, cruet, cuter, lucre, truce, ulcer
4 – celt, clue, cult, cure, curl, curt, cute, ecru

Puzzle 188
7 – imagine
6 – aiming, enigma, gamine
5 – anime, gamin, image, mange
4 – amen, game, magi, main, mane, mean, mien, mine, name

Puzzle 189
7 – nothing
6 – honing, noting, toning
5 – ingot, night, ninth, thing, thong
4 – hint, into, nigh, thin, ting, tong

Puzzle 190
7 – current
6 – return, turner
5 – cruet, curer, cuter, recur, rerun, truce, truer, tuner
4 – cure, curt, cute, ecru, rune, runt, true, tune, turn

Puzzle 191
7 – carrier
6 – racier
5 – airer, carer, crier, racer, rarer, ricer
4 – acre, care, race, rare, rear, rice

Puzzle 192
7 – hottest
5 – ethos, those, totes
4 – hoes, hose, host, shoe, shot, toes, tote, tots

Puzzle 193
7 – justice
6 – juices
5 – juice
4 – jest, jets, just, jute, juts

Puzzle 194
7 – project
5 – recto, repot, trope
4 – cope, core, crop, poet, pore, port, rope, rote, tore

Puzzle 195
7 – chicken
5 – check, chick, chink, cinch, niche
4 – chic, chin, hick, inch, neck, nice, nick

Puzzle 196
7 – offered
5 – defer, freed, offer
4 – doff, feed, ford, fore, free, reef

Puzzle 197
7 – locking
6 – coking
5 – clink
4 – kiln, kilo, king, lick, link, lock, nick

S
O
L
U
T
I
O
N
S

Puzzle 198
7 – chronic
6 – choric
5 – choir, cinch, conch, rhino
4 – chic, chin, horn, inch, rich

Puzzle 199
7 – varying
6 – grainy, raving
5 – angry, grain, gravy, rainy, rangy
4 – airy, grin, nary, rain, rang, ring, vary, yarn

Puzzle 200
7 – advisor
6 – avoids
5 – avoid, divas, visor, voids
4 – avid, diva, visa, void

Puzzle 201
7 – operate
5 – opera, orate, repot, trope
4 – atop, poet, pore, port, rope, rota, rote, tore

Puzzle 202
7 – blocked
6 – locked
5 – block, coked
4 – beck, bloc, clod, code, coed, coke, cold, deck, dock, lock

Puzzle 203
7 – heavily
5 – alive, halve, heavy
4 – evil, have, hive, levy, live, vale, veal, veil, vial, vile

Puzzle 204
7 – regular
6 – larger
5 – argue, glare, gruel, lager, large, regal
4 – ague, gale, gear, glue, guar, luge, rage, ragu, urge

Puzzle 205
7 – enforce
6 – confer, fencer
5 – fence, force
4 – fern, fore, free, reef

Puzzle 206
7 – earlier
6 – railer
5 – airer
4 – earl, lair, leer, liar, rail, rare, real, rear, reel, rile

Puzzle 207
7 – council
6 – uncoil
5 – colic, conic
4 – coil, coin, icon, lion, loci, loin

Puzzle 208
7 – booking
6 – booing
5 – bingo, bongo
4 – book, boon, knob, nook

Puzzle 209
7 – excepts, expects
6 – except, expect
5 – steep
4 – pest, pets, sect, seep, step, tees

Puzzle 210
7 – through
6 – though, trough
5 – grout, ought, rough, tough
4 – gout, thug, trug

Puzzle 211
7 – driving
6 – diving, riding, virgin
5 – grind, rigid
4 – ding, gird, grid, grin, rind, ring

Puzzle 212
7 – brother
6 – bother
5 – berth, borer, broth, throb
4 – bore, bort, both, herb, robe

Puzzle 213
7 – warning
6 – awning, waning
5 – awing, grain, wring
4 – gain, gnaw, grin, rang, ring, wing

Puzzle 214
7 – invalid
6 – inlaid
5 – anvil, divan, valid
4 – avid, dial, diva, ilia, laid, lain, land, nail, vain, vial

Puzzle 215
7 – popular
6 – poplar
5 – polar
4 – opal, palp, plop, pour, prop, pulp, pupa, purl

Puzzle 216
7 – twitter
6 – titter
5 – trite, write
4 – rite, tier, tire, weir, wire, writ

Puzzle 217
7 – variant
5 – atria, avian, tiara, train
4 – anti, aria, rain, vain

Puzzle 218
7 – sitting
6 – siting
5 – sting, stint, tings, tints
4 – gist, nits, ting, tins, tint, tits

Puzzle 219
7 – growers, regrows
6 – grower, regrow
5 – goers, gores, gorse, grows, ogres
4 – egos, ergo, ergs, goer, goes, gore, grew, grow, ogre

Puzzle 220
7 – housing
5 – suing, using
4 – gnus, guns, gush, hugs, hung, nous, onus, shun, snug, sung

Puzzle 221
7 – entered
6 – rented, tender
5 – enter, trend
4 – dene, dent, need, nerd, rend, rent, teen, tend, tern

Puzzle 222
7 – expired
5 – eider, pride, pried
4 – deep, deer, dire, drip, pied, reed, ride

Puzzle 223
7 – moments
6 – moment
5 – memos, motes, omens, smote, tomes
4 – memo, most, mote, omen, some, stem, tome

Puzzle 224
7 – lifting
6 – filing, tiling
5 – fling, flint, glint
4 – flit, gift, gilt, lift, lint, ting

Puzzle 225
7 – android
6 – inroad, ordain
5 – adorn, drain, nadir, radon
4 – darn, iron, rain, rind, roan

Puzzle 226
7 – figures
6 – figure, furies, griefs
5 – fires, fries, grief, serif
4 – figs, fire, firs, furs, fuse, rife, serf, surf

Puzzle 227
7 – calling
6 – lacing
5 – align, clang, cling, lilac
4 – call, clan, gall, gill, lain, nail

Puzzle 228
7 – formula
6 – armful, fulmar
5 – afoul, amour, flour, forum, mural
4 – alum, foul, four, furl, maul

Puzzle 229
7 – lessons, sonless
6 – lesson
5 – noses
4 – eons, lens, lone, nose, ones, sons

Puzzle 230
7 – visuals
6 – visual
5 – sails, vials, visas
4 – ails, lass, sail, visa

Puzzle 231
7 – battery
6 – betray, bratty, treaty
5 – batty, ratty, tarty, teary
4 – arty, bray, byre, byte, tray, tyre, year

Puzzle 232
7 – jointly
5 – joint
4 – into, jilt, join, lint, lion, loin, oily, tiny, toil

Puzzle 233
7 – advised
6 – advise
5 – divas, dived, dives, saved
4 – avid, diva, dive, save, vase, vied, vies, visa, vise

Puzzle 234
7 – finance
6 – canine, fiance
5 – inane
4 – acne, cafe, cane, face, fine, nice, nine

Puzzle 235
7 – wanting
6 – awning, waning
5 – awing, twain, twang
4 – gnaw, twig, twin, wait, want, wing

Puzzle 236
7 – portion
6 – proton
5 – print, troop
4 – iron, poor, port, riot, root, torn, trip

Puzzle 237
7 – totally
5 – allot, alloy, atoll, loyal, tally, total
4 – ally, alto, tall

Puzzle 238
7 – ordered
6 – eroded, redder
5 – erode, erred, odder, order
4 – deed, deer, doer, redo, reed, rode

Puzzle 239
7 – written
6 – winter
5 – rewin, twine, write
4 – newt, twin, twit, weir, went, wine, wire, wren, writ

Puzzle 240
7 – visited
6 – divest
5 – diets, dives, edits, sited, tides
4 – dies, diet, dive, edit, side, site, tide, tied, ties, vest, vets, vied, vies, vise

Puzzle 241
7 – nursery
6 – reruns
5 – nurse, rerun, runes
4 – rues, rune, runs, ruse, sure, urns, user

Puzzle 242
7 – premium
6 – immure, impure, umpire
5 – mimer, prime
4 – mime, mire, perm, prim, rime, rump

Puzzle 243
7 – accused
6 – accuse, caused
5 – cased, cause, sauce
4 – aced, aces, case, cued, cues, dace, scud

Puzzle 244
7 – foreign
6 – finger, fringe
5 – feign, finer, forge, grief, infer
4 – fern, fine, fire, fore, frog, rife

First published in 2023 by Ivy Press,
an imprint of The Quarto Group.
1 Triptych Place, London,
SE1 9SH, United Kingdom
T (0)20 7700 6700
www.Quarto.com

ISBN 978-0-7112-8700-6

10 9 8 7 6 5 4 3 2 1

Conceived, compiled and designed by Tim Dedopulos and Roland Hall

Printed and bound by CPI Group (UK) Ltd, Croydon, CR0 4YY

FSC
www.fsc.org
MIX
Paper | Supporting
responsible forestry
FSC® C171272